When Screams Become Whispers

T0054064

ADVANCED PRAISE

I've spent more than twenty years trying to design and test the efficacy of user group intervention for bipolar disorders. I've guided probably more than one hundred groups. Bob seems to have attended all of them!

This is the book of a bipolar disorder survivor that refused to be only that. A happy and functional living human willing to share his learned lessons with us. A gift.

I devoted all of my professional life to helping bipolar disordered people. I've got many books, projects and provisional drafts. I do not how Bob managed to get them and add a beautiful book from his own experience. He's living proof that you could actually live, not only survive, with bipolar. A must read for all sufferers, caregivers and friends.

Dr Francesc Colom, PsyD, PhD, MSc,
Senior Researcher at IMIM-Hospital del Mar, Barcelona, Spain,
co-author of *The Psychoeducation Manual for Bipolar Disorder*

The path to managing bipolar disorder doesn't have to be excruciating or even particularly difficult. To shine light for others, Bob Krulish shares every detail of his sometimes-harrowing adventures to create stability in his life. No matter how perplexing you find bipolar disorder for yourself or a loved, Bob's story will help relieve your guilt and give you powerful principles for success. From consulting rooms to courtrooms, and even encounters with Tony Robbins, "Bipolar Bob" provides something far better than hope. He shares how to find empathy for yourself so that you can transcend mere survival and start to thrive.

Anthony Metivier, author of *The Victorious Mind: How to Master Memory, Meditation and Mental Well-Being*

Bob Krulish bravely invites readers into some of his darkest days and most painful experiences as a person living with bipolar disorder. His remarkable story is proof that the human spirit has the power to transform pain and suffering into a life filled with hope and meaning. A must read!

Kristin Jarvis Adams, award-winning author of *The Chicken Who Saved Us: The Remarkable Story of Andrew and Frightful*

You are about to read of the roller-coaster life of a man that lived with undiagnosed bi-polar disorder well into his adult life. Bob's courage of writing this story may well save the lives of countless others that are either suffering the consequences of living with mental illness or are living with those that are. Once I started the book, I literally could not put it down until finished. The writing is captivating, and the message is profound. Read it yourself and then share it with many.

A. David Erlund, Sr. Partner, New York Life

Bob Krulish is an amazing human with an amazing story. His book, *When Screams Become Whispers* is a genuine portrayal of his loss, fight and ultimately, love for life. Through many trials and tribulations, this man is victorious over a mental illness that nearly destroyed him. Thank you, Bob Krulish, for taking the time and energy to share your story and make the world a healthier place. I'm grateful to know and work with you. Your friend, fan and skill coach.

Janina Johnson, Life Coach

Stories like Bob's need to be told. If kept inside, clinicians like me only get to see cross-sections of time, often when things are not going well. Brave books like this one are reminders that people have already traveled a long path before we join them on their journey.

Dr. Joshua Bess, Psychiatrist and Medical Director, Seattle NTC

For too long, a culture of shame and silence has stigmatized mental health. The vivid and honest story that Bob Krulish tells of his struggle with bipolar disorder, and what an incorrect diagnosis cost him, is a beautiful example of how we explode that stigma. Bob brings laughter and humor to his story so that we can relate and understand without losing sight of the deep suffering that mental health problems can cause.

Manka Dhingra, Washington State Senator
and Mental Health Advocate

With When Screams Become Whispers, Bob Krulish not only demonstrates that there is hope for ending the suffering caused by bipolar disorder, he reminds us how important it is to have stories like his—stories of possibilities, empowerment and wellness—told well and told more often. This is an excellent and powerful work of advocacy on behalf of those suffering from a debilitating illness and those who care for them.

John Capecci, co-author,
Living Proof: Telling Your Story to Make a Difference

Bob's pioneering work reveals people living with mental health challenges for who they really are--people of incredible valor and undaunted resolve, heroes among us. *When Screams Become Whispers* will engender empathy and understanding in readers who have not walked this road. And it will carry special meaning for those on their own journey with bipolar disorder. It's one thing to tell a person with a new diagnosis that there is hope; it's another thing entirely to show them. Thank you, Bob, for reminding us all that no one has fallen too far to recover.

Lauren Davis, Washington State Representative
and Founding Director of Washington Recovery Alliance

Bob Krulish is a living example of a mental health triumph. A hero's journey. That is to say, he somehow has strength of character and determination that can withstand the extraordinary trials, struggles, and ups and downs that are the roller-coaster of living with a mental health challenge.

His honesty, bravery, grit, and humor through it all – his humanness – is part of the glue that unites us in dispelling long-held stigma.

Caroline Garry, Principal, Caroline Garry Branding

I've worked with Bob as an advocate and storyteller for several years. What strikes me most about him is his honesty and his humor. He's one of those rare people who can talk about the darkest of times and make you unafraid and not sad for him, you feel comfortable and comforted. Plus, he's hilarious

Bill Bernat, TEDx Speaker and Founder of Stay Awesome

I wish every hard thing in life came with a book like this. If you or someone you love has bipolar you need to read it. Bob tells you what life is like living with bipolar and then he gives you hope for how to deal with it. Listen and learn from doctors and therapists but keep this book in your back pocket. It's what you'll turn to when you need to be reminded that you're not alone.

Paul Currington, Host, Fresh Ground Stories

WHEN SCREAMS BECOME WHISPERS

One Man's Inspiring Victory Over Bipolar Disorder

BOB KRULISH
with Alee Anderson

NEW YORK

LONDON • NASHVILLE • MELBOURNE • VANCOUVER

When Screams Become Whispers

One Man's Inspiring Victory Over Bipolar Disorder

Published in New York, New York, by Morgan James Publishing. Morgan James is a trademark of Morgan James, LLC. www.MorganJamesPublishing.com

ISBN 9781631953132 paperback
ISBN 9781631953149 eBook
Library of Congress Control Number: 2020945456

Cover & Interior Design by:
Christopher Kirk
www.GFSstudio.com

Morgan James is a proud partner of Habitat for Humanity Peninsula and Greater Williamsburg. Partners in building since 2006.

Get involved today! Visit
MorganJamesPublishing.com/giving-back

To all those who struggle, and to those who care for them.

Never give up, never give up.

A NOTE FROM THE AUTHOR

This book is my own story of life with a mental illness. I hope my account will encourage others to seek professional diagnoses and treatment.

The biggest challenge to writing this memoir was to choose the right combination of events to bring my story to life. As my memory is sometimes fallible it was sometimes difficult to remember the details of each moment in the midst of traumatic situations. Dialogue is approximate in some places. What you hold in your hands is the story as I experienced it.

For reasons of privacy, the names and details of a few minor characters have been changed. This book contains advice and information relating to mental health care. It should not be used to replace the advice of a trained mental health professional.

Bob Krulish

TABLE OF CONTENTS

LETTER FROM A GRATEFUL CLIENT

I met Bob Krulish in January of 2016; he was a featured speaker for a NAMI (National Alliance on Mental Illness) "In our Own Voices" presentation. I sat in the audience and heard Bob's story of his life with Bipolar disease but quite honestly, I didn't completely believe him. He was way too put together for the story he told. It just didn't seem possible that this man who was speaking in front of me about the awful life experiences he had as a result of untreated Bipolar disease, could have the insight that he was sharing that night.

I spent the next 3 weeks researching him. I did this because "He was too good to be true." I had prayed long and hard for God to drop someone in my path that could help me, help my mentally ill child. Bob appeared to be this person but in a much bigger way. Finally, after doing my sleuthing, I called the program coordinator who had set up the "In Our Own Voices" presentation and asked her, "Is he for real? Does he really HAVE bipolar disease?" The line went quiet for about fifteen seconds (I think she was composing herself) and then she came back on the line and said, "Yes, he is the real deal."

I immediately called Bob, told him the truth of what I had done, and we began a connection that has involved Bob wearing many hats: individual counselor, family counselor, insightful peer to my son, life coach, and dare I say, friend. Here is how he has helped me in just one small year.

Let me set the stage first. My son had gone on and off medicine over the years (it has been 8 years since his initial diagnosis). In January of 2017, he had gone off all medicine and become more and more manic as the year progressed.

I was naïve to initially recognize that my son had gone off his meds. It quickly became apparent and by April he was threatening me and being very verbally abusive. My child was a master of manipulation and the definition of normal had skewed so much that I did not know where to turn. I had talked with Bob a few times before this, but it was then that I called Bob, asking for reality checks. Bob seemed to speak as though he were in my son's head. The words that came out of his mouth describe the behavior I was seeing in my son. It was these discussions that really cemented the fact that Bob does indeed have Bipolar disease because his advice at some points appeared to be counter-intuitive but with 20/20 hindsight now, they were always the right bits of advice. In July of 2017 Bob started counseling my family (Peer to Family). Teaching all of us (except our sick son) about Bipolar disease, what triggers to avoid, how to talk, how to act, how to try to live with our son and brother. Bob's willingness to be vulnerable and tell his own personal stories helped my family and I to begin to understand that our loved one was not a monster; helped us all to feel validated in our feelings (and let us own them and deal with them in our own time), opened our hearts to the compassion we all so needed but couldn't grasp through our own hurt and gave us concrete information which developed skills within each of us to be able to show support to our loved one. Bob's research, outside of his own experience with Bipolar, makes him a resource of 'cliff-note" proportion to hundreds of books. He has summarized this information into hand-outs and weekly lessons that he used during our counseling sessions.

At the end of August, our loved one entered a mental illness treatment facility in another state. Bob became even more helpful because the focus went from dealing with the crisis-level day-to-day interactions with our manic son/brother to "How do we as the family members begin to try to heal ourselves?" The ill one was in residential treatment – he was bound to get better. But, how would we? I remember the first family counseling session after our loved one had entered the treatment facility, (everything happened so fast that I had no time to tell Bob that our son was gone) the call started off as a continuation of the lesson plan Bob had prepared but quickly changed due to the family members being in need of help, how would we ever re-set? We felt PTSD, fear, and hate. Bob listened and then wisely suggested we redirect our work and focus on the family. Over the next three months Bob worked with us by having weekly family talk therapy sessions. Each person was given time to vent and ultimately release their pent-up emotions. By the end of November, the sessions progressed into, how would we prepare ourselves for our loved-one's 5-day visit at Christmas? Bob coached us on talking skills, words to use and not use to communicate with our son/brother when he returned. Bob was able to articulate his own experience after coming off a hot-brain, extended manic cycle and his teachings were paramount to our success as a family in coming together over those days in a supportive yet non-codependent manner.

The visit was beautiful for everyone. Fast-forward to the end of January 2018. We brought our son home from treatment and after 5 months he was in a much better place, but Bob continued to educate us to "Think of it as though he has just gone through a big dose of Chemotherapy treatment for cancer. The cancer is in remission, but the body is wiped out. Let him slowly get his feet under himself." This would be the antithesis of how I would have thought to treat my son. I might be more inclined to crack the whip and encourage/suggest/insist that he go out and at least get a job now that he was home, not going to school and basically hanging out. What I see now is that my son needed this time to slowly work with his psychiatrist to tweak the medicines he came home with (his brain is continuing to cool down and doesn't need as strong of dosages now and so he and the doctor are titrating back the meds), re-learn how to integrate back into society, and make tiny steps forward. Bob is fortunately coaching my husband and I now on how to be supportive to our son - how to delete the words "should, ought, must" from our vocabulary to him, while feeling comfortable and accepting that we are not being manipulated by our son.

I honestly do not want to think of where our family would be right now if it wasn't for having met Bob Krulish. I am afraid that we would not be connected to our loved one and that would make all of us sick. Now Bob is befriending our son and wants to be a resource to him (Peer to Peer) to help our son learn how to manage his illness and keep it in remission. Bob wants to provide this kind of help to as many people as he possibly can. Through videos, webinars, speaking engagements, a book about Bob's life and one-on-one counseling; Bob Krulish is going to offer his insight and personal life experience to the world. Bob's goal is to ease the pain and suffering of those affected by mental illness and those caught in the ripple effect that it produces.

He **IS** the REAL DEAL!

Sue R.

FOREWORD

R eaders of *When Screams Become Whispers* are transported to a fourth dimension of human experience that is very rarely seen much less understood. We are enlightened and inspired. Bob Krulish reveals, with powerful and evocative prose, the mind and heart of people living with Bipolar Disorder. His empathy, wisdom and encouragement speaks to the sufferer and their loved ones who have been forced to ride the explosive rollercoaster that is untreated bipolar disorder. This book is much more than a journey into the experience of a family whose ill loved ones have been eclipsed by mental illness. It is a hopeful tale that offers hard won wisdom for persons living with bipolar disorder. *When Screams Become Whispers* is a must read for anyone who has a desire to understand the experience of mental illness and for those living with it—both the person with the diagnosis and their family. This is a hopeful book that has my highest, wholehearted, praise.

Xavier Amador, Ph.D.
Bestselling author of *I Am Not Sick, I Don't Need Help!*

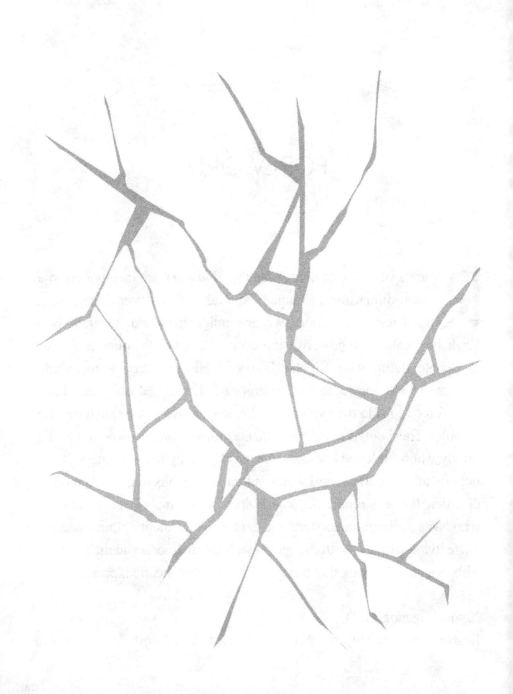

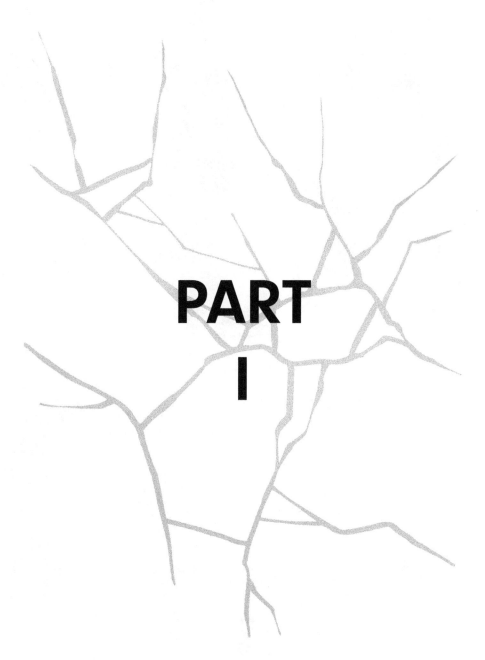

PART
I

Chapter 1

BROKEN GLASS

The sound of shattering glass startles me. My eyes dart from my algebra homework to the bedroom door. The yelling has been steady for about an hour, and I know that the sound of breaking glass typically means the fight has reached its peak. Now, things will ebb and flow until the argument officially ends. There will be sobbing, then low chatter, more crying, one more burst of yelling, then silence, sometimes punctuated by a slamming door. I know this rhythm well.

I look around the room, checking for signs that the crashing sound has woken my brother or sister. Kryse is asleep with a pillow over her head, her tiny body outstretched, left arm dangling over the side. Rik is sprawled out like a starfish, his feet nearly grazing the bottom of his mattress. Neither has so much as stirred. I'm not surprised. The sound of our parents fighting has been the steady background noise in our lives as long as I can remember. It provides the soundtrack most nights as we three kids go about our own routines. We brush our teeth, button our pajamas, then whisper good night as we tuck into our beds and huddle under covers, each of us eventually fumbling for a comic book and a flashlight. There, in our room, each bed has its own illuminated hump, a cocoon of safety and solace in moments of madness. On rare occasions, our door flies open and one of us is called to the carpet. Typically, we're asked to confirm a fact, defend an action, and once in a while, to apologize for something that we did, maybe even months earlier. Sometimes there's hair pulling, slapping, and holes punched in walls. On the worst nights, things escalate fast. My dad's eyes are wild, his speech hurried. Once, as we watched, he threw my mom down in front of the stove, sat on top of her, and yelled into her face, as if she wouldn't learn unless he forced her to ingest his words. When I cried out, he stood up and ran toward me. He picked me up like a rag doll and threw me midair across the room. Fights don't always end that way, but it's happened enough that my stomach flips when the volume rises sharply.

My desk lamp casts soft yellow light on my notebook, the pages strewn with numbers and symbols that were once foreign to me. Now, they are the exact opposite. They comfort me, offering the opportunity to get something right—absolutely, unequivocally, completely right. Some people feel comfortable in areas that are gray. Not me. I like black and white.

I have six equations to finish before I can to go to bed. I start in on the next one, $5xy - xy = 4xy$. As I write, I can't help but strain to see if I can hear any more conversation. It's quiet enough that the scratching of my lead pencil on the paper seems sharp. Then I hear it.

Slam.

It's the front door, not one of the interior doors, so I know what's next. The engine of my dad's Lincoln roars on, revs three times; there is a flash as the headlights illuminate our bedroom while he backs down the driveway, then the light fades, the tires screech, and he drives off. It is dark again. I don't know where he goes and I don't care. His absence brings silence and some measure of relief. It's over for the night.

I creep to the door, stepping carefully over the floorboard I know is creaky. I grab the knob and pull, easing the door open. As I step into the hallway, I hear the soft, muffled sounds of my mom crying. I make my way toward the living room, my feet sinking into the soft shag carpet with each step. I round the corner, squinting as the bright light hits my eyes. My mom is sitting on the edge of the sofa, her nightgown grazing the floor. She is leaning forward, hands covering her eyes as her shoulders move up and down softly with each quiet sob. Broken glass is scattered on the floor near the fireplace.

"Mom?" I call softly.

She jumps, then says, "Bobby, what are you doing up? It's late." She turns away and wipes the tears from her eyes, as if there's any chance she can hide it.

"I was finishing my algebra homework. Are you…?"

"I'm fine," she says, feigning a smile. She opens her arms, welcoming me into a warm hug. My mom is soft, especially compared to my dad, who is hard in every way. He is athletic and muscular, his arms often crossed in front of him. He never offers any measure of tenderness, no kisses or hugs. The best we can hope for is a firm handshake or a slight nod of approval if we do something he likes.

"Okay, then," I say, pulling myself out of her arms. "I guess I'll get back to it."

"Good, but let me tell you something first," she says softly, taking my hands. She looks into my eyes. "Don't say anything to Rik or Kryse yet, but I think it may be time for us to make a change. Your dad's been talking about it for a long time."

"What do you mean?"

"Well, he says I'm not happy, that I'm tired, that I could use help. I feel okay, but he makes a good point, we have a lot going on. You know, he's been talking a lot about going to Albuquerque, near aunt Jo."

"Like, for a visit?"

"No. I think we need to leave for good. I think it's the only way things will get better. He's right. I could use the support and I know my moods don't help. School is almost out for summer anyway; it could be the right time." She pauses for a moment, then sighs and continues, "He seems to really want this…for us."

I'm not sure what to say, so I don't say anything. I know New Mexico is the last place we should go, but I try to muster a smile as my mom gestures that I should go back to my room. As I leave, she stands and straightens her nightgown, then walks toward the kitchen to grab her dustpan and broom. I can't imagine what it would be like to pack all our things, get in the car and drive, leaving Long Island and everything we know behind. I walk into my room then straight to my bookshelf and run my hands along the spines of books until I find my atlas. I flip to the map of New Mexico and trace my finger along the fat highway connecting Albuquerque and Santa Fe. There would be just sixty-five miles between our family and my dad's biggest weakness. How can my mom possibly think this is something we should do to make our family stronger?

I close the book and put it back on the shelf, trying to shake the worry that's settled into the pit of my stomach. I wonder if my dad really would be happier in the desert, and for a moment I picture us driving golf balls under the beating sun, dust coating our pants as we play together for the very first time. But I know it's silly to even think about. After all, he is hard in every way, and his heart is no exception. Well, when it comes to us anyway.

I settle back into my desk chair, the house now silent as I etch my final answers onto the white sheet of paper in lead so dark it might as well be black.

Chapter 2

A-

I unplug my lamp and start to gather the pens, pencils, and bits of scrap paper covering my desk. There is a box on the floor next to me, the top open like a hungry mouth waiting to swallow the contents of my life. I begin to pile papers and remember that I have a stack in my backpack that I need to unload. I unzip the bag and roll my eyes, remembering what will greet me. I take a deep breath and grab the wrinkled paper nestled on top—my algebra final. I flatten it against my desk. The grade written on it in red pen glares up at me. A-.

"Need another one?" my mom asks, walking into my room with an empty box in hand.

"Maybe," I reply. "Just put it down somewhere."

She places the box on my stripped bed, crosses the room, and kisses the top of my head. "Another A. Great job."

"No," I snap. "Look." I drive my pointer finger into the minus. "I could've done better. I'm such an idiot."

"I don't understand why you do that to yourself." She tousles my hair. "An A is an A is an A. Just finish up. Your father wants to be out of here before lunchtime."

"Minus," I whisper to myself as my mom's footsteps fade. I focus my attention back on the paper. The minus sign stares at me, a tiny reminder of my total inadequacy. One decimal point in the wrong place caused me to get a problem wrong. One. I remember how awful that school day was. I had taken the test after a sleepless night thanks to my dad forcing me to sit at the dining table with him as he ranted and raved about something I can't even remember now. The next day in class, I found myself nodding off while I tried to concentrate on the test, the sweet silence in the room causing my eyes to droop. I was making stupid mistakes that day. Over and over, I kept placing decimals one point off. Before I passed my paper to the teacher, I double-checked my work, then triple-checked it to be sure. I still didn't catch this one dumb mistake and it ruined my streak of perfect grades right as I was about to cross the finish line. Bob Krulish, also known as The Answer Key, got an A-.

But next time. Next time I take a test, it'll be at a new school in Albuquerque. It was just a week ago, hours after the glass shattered against the fireplace, when my parents officially decided we'd move. This rash decision perfectly characterizes my parents' relationship. My father is irrational and fanciful; he makes huge claims, sweeping state-ments, and swears he knows what's right. He can be charming when he needs to be and can manipulate anyone into not only doing what he wants but into thinking it's their idea. My mom is sweet and kind, maybe even a little weak. She does what he wants to keep him happy, for even just a while. It never works, and I know deep down that it won't work this time, but I let myself hold on to hope like a childhood plaything I know I've outgrown.

I make my way through the maze of boxes and head to the kitchen for a glass of water. I pass my mom wrapping the last of her ceramic figurines in the living room as Kryse and Rik play jacks on the floor.

There is clanking and clattering in the kitchen as my dad stacks the dishes one by one. He is whistling "Proud Mary" by Creedence Clearwater Revival and I stop in the doorway. The early morning sun is streaming through the window above the sink, casting golden light on the bare tiled floor. The table is gone, as is the small tattered rug that had sat in front of the fridge, and there is a light, oblong spot on the wall where our Kit-Cat clock once hung. My mom brushes past me and walks up to my dad, who smiles at her as she takes a few sheets of newspaper from the counter. I know that smile. It's the sweet, satisfied smile of someone who has gotten his way. My mom turns with the sheets of newspaper in hand and walks back toward the living room, softly touching my shoulder as she passes. She smells like Ivory soap and maple syrup. It dawns on me that if someone were to peek through the window at this exact moment, they'd think we were a happy family.

As I walk across the kitchen floor, my sneaker catches the tile, making a piercing squeak. My dad looks up from the dishes and stops whistling.

"Your room better be packed if you're taking a break."

"I'm almost done," I respond. "Can I get a drink of water?"

"Go right ahead," he says, motioning at the faucet.

I reach out, grasp the cold metal handle, and pull it toward me. I cup my hand beneath the chilly water spilling from the faucet and bring it to my mouth. I feel his eyes on me but remain laser-focused and take a large gulp. I finish, shake off the remaining water into the sink, then wipe my hands on my pants. Just before I turn to leave, our eyes meet and my stomach flips.

"Your last day of school was yesterday, right?"

"Yeah."

"So? Grades?"

"No report card yet, but I got my algebra test back. A." I hesitate, then add, "minus."

He holds my gaze, then starts, "Well." A slight, crooked smile flickers across his face before he continues, "There's always next time. Finish up in there. We're packing the trailer the minute I finish with this crap." Then he turns back to the counter and picks up whistling right where he left off.

I walk quickly back into my room and head straight for the test. I grab it, ball it up, and shove it deep into a trash bag under my desk. I sit down hard in my chair and ball my fists, pressing my nails sharply into my palms. I had been on a perfect streak. A+ after A+ after A+. My dad never celebrated those successes, but he always offered a "Well done, son." And sometimes, if I showed him a good grade after his second nightly martini, he'd give me a firm pat on the back. I remind myself that I don't need his love. I don't need his approval. I don't need anything from him. Right now, what I need to do is to finish packing so I can pile into the car with my family and drive into the unknown. I think back to the A- and hope that I can muster the intelligence to pack without ruining everything I own.

Chapter 3

ALMOST THERE

I am startled awake as we hit a pothole, and I whack my head on the window. The trailer hitched to my dad's Lincoln continues to follow the car like an eager friend. It casts a dark shadow over the back of the car, which is increasingly welcome as the desert sun beats down, heating the glass enough to sting my forehead when I press my head against it. The front windows are open, sending swathes of warm air streaming through the car.

As we've driven through seven states, I've watched the landscape turn from one I know well to one that feels totally alien. On Long Island, the trees were big and billowy, almost fluffy like clouds. The grass is green and lush—well manicured as if someone had expertly cared for each blade. The farther we drove, the more spread out the houses became and the lower and more sparse the greenery seemed. With each mile, the landscape continued to morph until we crossed into New Mexico. Here, the land is flat, flanked by mountains on nearly all sides. The sky seems wide and blue, sharply contrasted by the rocky sand that stretches for miles. The greenery is squat and shrubby and looks completely brittle, as if it could catch fire in the blink of an eye. If I didn't know any better, I'd think we'd crash-landed on Mars.

Kryse's leg is touching mine and has been for long enough that a pool of our combined sweat is forming. I look over to tell her off and notice she's asleep with her mouth open slightly. My brother is on the other side of her staring blankly out the window. I decide not to wake my sister but instead nudge her toward Rik as I inch closer to the door. We've driven thirty hours in three days and are all ready for space. I close my eyes and imagine running fast, my legs aching, lungs burning, arms pumping as I zoom away from the car and everyone in it.

Though moving across the country feels like a big deal, the trip hasn't been that bad. We stopped along the way at motels in Indiana and Oklahoma and ate greasy truck stop burgers both nights, picnic style on the floor of our room. My dad's mood has been light and breezy. He's cracked a few jokes and even laughed and hoisted my sister onto his shoulders as my brother and I wrestled playfully at a rest stop in Missouri while we waited for my mom to buy snacks. When she came out of the store and headed toward us, she broke into a jog as if she couldn't wait to join the fun that she hoped would be our family's new normal.

Now, Dad is driving and Mom is sitting in the passenger seat, humming softly to herself. This, I think, is the perfect metaphor for their relationship: my dad in the driver's seat, my mom totally content to be along for the ride. The map rests on her lap, ready for the moment when my dad will begin barking for directions and banging the dashboard in frustration when she doesn't let him know soon enough when his turns are coming up.

My mind begins to wander to our new life and what things will be like when we get to our new home. I wonder what my new friends will be like, how quickly I'll move up in the ranks on the golf team, and how long it'll take me to build a reputation as Bob Krulish—The Answer

Key. With my A- firmly in the rearview mirror, I hope it won't take long. I'm looking forward to getting our new routine down because that's what I like: routine. Simple, ordinary, easy-to-follow. Our old life might not have been perfect, but it was perfectly predictable. We kids would go to school, stay for after-school activities, then head home together as the sun set. We'd walk into the house, and when the front door slammed shut, our mom would come in from the garage, where she'd been working on ceramics. She'd greet us with clay-coated hands and remind us to hang up our jackets and put our shoes where they go. Then we'd settle in to do our homework, the smell of pot roast, meatballs, or chicken cutlets hanging in the air.

My dad had worked as an architect in New York City. He'd commuted by Long Island Railroad every morning and spent his days designing high-rise buildings and luxury homes. Some nights, we'd pick him up at the Hempstead train station. My mom would carefully ease the car into a parking spot before opening the door, getting out, and scurrying to the other side of the car, sinking into the passenger seat as the train pulled in. We could always tell what kind of mood my dad was in by the way he walked to the car. Sometimes he'd step off the train with a smile. His gait was wide, and he'd stride toward the car in a soft fluid motion. On those nights, he'd be in conversation with fellow passengers and would wave to us as he made his way through the crowd. On other nights, he seemed to explode out of the train car as if he'd been pressed against the wall for the duration of the ride, ready to pounce on the platform as soon as the clunky doors slid open. On those nights, his feet would stomp against the pavement as he walked with purpose toward our idling car. He'd gesticulate angrily as he bumped past fellow commuters. When he grabbed at the driver's-side door of our car, we knew what was coming. His briefcase would land with a hard thump on my mom's lap, swiftly followed by his body sinking sharply into the driver's seat. He'd be cursing under his breath while the car was still idling.

The smell of Old Spice mingled with the smell of cigarette smoke and spilled whiskey as it wafted off of his jacket and into the back seat. My sister would grab my hand and squeeze so tight I could feel the steady beat of her pulse beneath my fingers.

Although the nights when he returned full of rage were awful, they weren't the worst. On the worst nights, we'd get to the train station and he simply wouldn't be there. His regular train would pull in, brakes squealing urgently, the smell of exhaust heavy in the air. We'd wait until the crowd thinned, then dissipated entirely, and we'd sit for a few moments in silence before heading home. My mom would make small talk as she softly dabbed at her tears. When we got home, we would eat dinner in silence, then finish our homework and go to bed, while my mom cried herself to sleep.

My dad always had an excuse for his absence. Sometimes, he'd say he had a dinner meeting; other times he'd claim that he got caught up in his work or that he'd had an extremely important deadline to meet. But there was one excuse that he favored—one that he seemed to know little kids would eat up. Although my dad did maintain that he went into the city every day to design those high-rise buildings and luxury homes, that wasn't the only job he claimed to keep. He said he was also a CIA agent who would be called on periodically to carry out various dangerous missions. He could never turn down a mission nor could he ever tell anyone about them, even after they were complete. That, he claimed, was why he would sometimes disappear without explanation. Of course he couldn't call and let us know where he would be, because those details were classified. It was also why he always carried a concealed weapon. The night he told Kryse, Rik, and me about his work with the CIA, we stared at him wide-eyed as he lifted his pant leg so we could see the gun strapped to his calf. Then he leaned back in his chair, lifted an eyebrow, and said, "But you can't tell anyone, because they'll kill us all if my cover is blown." Even though he had the telltale signs of madness in his voice, I remember the cold feeling of fear rushing through my body, making my knees feel weak beneath the weight of the secret my dad had just shared. I didn't know what to think.

Even now, looking at the back of my dad's head, his blond hair flopping in the wind, I don't know for certain whether he believed he worked for the CIA or whether it was a lie crafted to scare us out of questioning his motives. It seems crazy to make a baseless claim that you have a job with the CIA…so crazy that I can't imagine someone making it up. There are also a lot of things about my dad that make him seem like he really could have been a secret agent. He is in good shape and could have certainly handled the physical strain. He doesn't have many friends, so there is little risk that he'd leak sensitive information. He is always on high alert, ready to defend himself at a moment's notice. Then there's the fact that he disappears several times a month without explanation. Although, there is one alternate explanation I know of for at least some of the nights he'd been gone.

It all came to the surface during one of my mom and dad's arguments. Their fighting had been particularly animated that night, my mom crying out loudly, my dad hitting the wall more than once. Rik and Kryse were both much younger then and were startled awake at one point. I had to work to keep them both quiet and eventually shepherded them into my bed with me so I could distract them with a long story. As our parents continued to shout back and forth, my mom got up and walked toward their bedroom and my dad followed, stomping his feet and shouting. He grabbed her and pushed her against the wall right outside our bedroom door.

"Don't you walk away from me," he'd hissed through clenched teeth.

"I just can't believe you've been with someone else." She could barely catch her breath. "And Maureen was my friend."

I'd pulled the covers over all three of us and thought about Maureen. My dad had taken us horseback riding with her on a day when my mom had gone shopping with her sister. I recall thinking that he and Maureen seemed like friends. It was odd to see him with a friend, and I remember having fun with this version of my dad I'd never seen before. Afterward he'd taken us out for ice cream and chuckled lovingly instead of yelling at my sister when she left the ice cream shop covered in hot fudge.

Now, in the front seat, my mom reaches into her purse and pulls out a mirror and a tube of lipstick. As she applies it, her wedding ring catches my eye. It is tight on her finger, creating an indentation that looks permanently pressed into her skin. It reminds me of the hold my dad has on her. He is wrapped so tightly around her that she's been permanently changed.

After the night my mom found out about the affair, he'd promised it would stop. But, of course, it continued, maybe even intensified. I'd watched my mom drive herself crazy, not only crying when he didn't return home, but pacing the floor, biting her nails, and periodically picking up the receiver to make sure the phone was still working. Of course, it was working fine, but it never rang with him on the other end.

Soon, it was revealed that my mom wasn't the only one who was being driven crazy by the affair. Maureen's husband, Sal, found out. He was enraged, astonished that Maureen would betray him and their kids that way. Maureen promised it would stop, the same way my dad did. When things continued, Sal promised to put a stop to things once and for all by picking up their family and moving them to Santa Fe, New Mexico. Of course, Sal never imagined that my dad would find a way to follow.

Once Maureen and her family left, my mom's moods changed. She went back to being her sweet, warm, present self. She no longer had a reason to pace the floors, bite her nails, or obsessively check the phone. My dad's presence became steadier, and there were far fewer nights when he didn't return home. This, however, came with its own set of challenges, because his moods were even more explosive than normal. From the moment he threw his bag onto my mom's lap until the moment his head hit the pillow, we were on high alert, ready for a nuclear bomb to detonate. And when it did, the fights were ugly. He would hurl insults, make threats, and call us awful names. Yet, as horrible as he was to us, we never stopped loving him and yearning for change. Kryse wished on every birthday candle that he would one day treat her like a princess, and Rik would have given anything to toss a football with him or play a round of golf. My dad actually did do those things with me, but it came at a cost. To remain in his favor, I had to keep my grades way up, I had to continue to be impeccably behaved, and I had to maintain high standards in everything I did. I was the "chosen one" and received special treatment, but it was contingent on me being someone he could brag about around the water cooler at work. Although the way he treated me was far from good, it was vastly better than the way he treated Rik and Kryse. As a result, they stuck closely together while pushing me away.

Now, the closer we get to our new home, I can't help but wonder whether there is even a slight chance that this change will be good for our family. I can't shake the feeling that there was no way New Mexico was a coincidence. In all likelihood, my dad designed things this way so he and Maureen could pick up right where they left off. Sixty-five miles is nothing—barely an hour without traffic. My gut tells me there's no way that wasn't part of the plan. I just have to take it a day at a time, hope for the best but brace for the worst.

I stare at my mom's curly hair billowing in the wind. Tiny flecks of gray catch the light, offering bright shimmers that look like bits of silver glitter. She reaches her hand over and places it on my dad's shoulder. He deliberately shrugs it off, motioning toward the road as if to indicate that he needs to concentrate.

As we pull off the highway, my sister wakes up and rubs her eyes. "Are we there yet?" she asks.

My mom fumbles with the map, her finger tracing our route. She pauses, then replies, "Almost."

Chapter 4

THE ANSWER KEY

Heat prickles my skin as I lie beneath the beating sun. My eyes are closed and my hands are clasped together behind my head. Sweat is forming beneath my hair and rolling down my spine. My legs are outstretched in front of me, and each time I switch positions, the lounge chair I'm resting on gives them a sharp pinch.

"Cannonball!" Rik yells as he runs toward the pool. He leaps as soon as his feet hit the pool's edge and tucks into a tight ball. I shut my eyes tightly as his body hits the cool water, sending droplets hurtling through the air. Several land on my leg with one loud splat. Laughter erupts from the pool deck as my brother comes up for air.

I open my eyes to see my parents sitting in the shade, my dad's bare chest glistening as if he's just rubbed oil on himself. My mom is in a long, flowing dress that covers her entire body and her hair is tucked into a swimming cap. She and my dad are wearing matching aviator sunglasses, which they bought at a gas station when we crossed into New Mexico. My aunt is placing paper plates around the table on the pool deck while my uncle flips burgers and rotates hot dogs on the grill. Kryse is wearing goggles and sitting on the edge of the pool in an inner tube, carefully dangling her feet into the water. The smell of charcoal hangs in the hot, dry summer air.

It's been three weeks since we moved into our new house in Albuquerque and, so far, things seem almost too good to be true. The house itself is nicer than our old one. It's a brick ranch-style home with wood floors and a big burned yard that my dad is trying to revive with sprinklers and obsessive upkeep. When I wake up in the morning, he is often walking an imaginary grid across the lawn, a spike aerator in one hand and a cup of coffee in the other. We kids still share a room, but it's bigger than the one we grew up sharing. The mood in our house has been lighter. My dad found work quickly, comes home happy almost every night, and he even makes time to hit golf balls with me once every so often to help me get ready to try out for the golf team. My mom has been spending time with her sister and has set up her ceramics studio in the garage. School hasn't started yet, so we are spending time riding bikes, exploring, and trying to make friends in the neighborhood. Rik and Kryse often go off to do their own thing, leaving me alone in the yard to practice my golf swing or to review formulas, theorems, and equations that I want to have memorized by the time school starts. Sometimes I hear distant laughter and feel the pull of sadness that comes with being left out, but it's okay. I get why they're close, and if I'm honest, I wouldn't trade my position as my dad's chosen one for anything at all.

Now, the sizzling on the grill is beginning to fade, so I can tell my uncle is almost done cooking. My dad chugs the last of the beer in the sweaty can he is holding, puts it down on the table with a hollow tap, stands and walks toward the deep end of the pool.

"Okay, everyone," he says loudly, stepping onto the diving board. "Feast your eyes on this!"

My mom stands and pushes her aviators onto her head and shields her eyes with her right hand to get a better look. Rik swims out of the way, propping himself up on the side of the pool next to Kryse. My dad jumps hard with both feet and flings himself in the air. It looks like he's about to perform the perfect dive, but on his last jump, his foot slips and he falls face-first into the pool. There is a heavy splash as he hits the water, sending a wave crashing onto the cement. When he comes up for air, everyone is silent. This is a moment when things could go south—a failure of any kind is enough to send my dad into a rage, but a public one usually causes him to stomp off in a huff before spending the rest of the day exploding at every little thing. He brushes his wet golden hair back with his right hand. He clenches his jaw, looking around the pool as if he's calculating his next move. Then, to our surprise, he bursts into laughter. Within seconds, everyone around the pool drops their shoulders and starts to laugh too. I am laughing so hard, my stomach muscles begin to ache. He gets out of the pool and shrugs his shoulders. "I guess I won't make the Olympic team, huh?"

As the laughter subsides, I turn and put my damp feet on the cement with a hiss. My mom motions for us to get ready to eat, so I jog toward the table in the shade, not wanting my bare feet to remain on the concrete for more than a second at a time. As my uncle piles a scorched hot dog and a juicy cheeseburger onto my plate, I reach for the cold potato salad and scoop some into the empty spot next to the meat. I find a seat at the table and settle in before reaching behind me to plunge my hand into the icy cooler to grab a Coke. A couple drops of frigid water fall from the frosty can onto my lap and I try for a moment to remember what cold weather feels like.

I look around the table at my family as they finish serving themselves. Rik and Kryse playfully nudge one another as my dad pulls the tab on another beer. I've seen him smile more in the past few weeks than I have in my entire life. Yet, as relaxed as I have started to feel in our new routine, something keeps me from letting go completely. I wonder if the threat of things going back to the way they used to be will always loom. Sometimes I'll be reading in my room and hear a door slam and I'll stand reflexively and run to the doorway, straining to hear whether or not they're fighting. Other times, I'll catch my dad's eye, and he'll look at me with a furrowed brow, as if he's about to call me a name or tell me I'm doing something stupid—but instead, he'll look away or even crack a small, almost imperceptible smile. My mom has been happy. Singing in the shower, tickling the bottom of our feet, cooking delicious, heartwarming food. Her face is relaxed; her eyes, no longer perpetually puffy and red, are now sparkly and bright all the time. This is the life I want for my mom and for us: sun kissed and smiling, finally enjoying one another the way a family should.

<hr />

The first day of school is always weird, but the first day at a new school is exceptionally nerve-racking. I still feel the summer on my skin, but the stress of a new school year revives the familiar tension in my shoulders. My stomach is flip-flopping all over the place as I walk through the doors of my new school and get swept up in a sea of kids who all seem like they know where they're going. The school smells like new paint and pencil shavings, which I find oddly comforting. My main goal today is to prevent myself from looking like an idiot while I get the lay of the land.

I tuck my thumbs beneath the straps of my backpack and try to look casual as I figure out where my homeroom class could be. I'm looking for Mr. Foster's room and I know it has to be nearby. I try to spot kids close to my age so I can see where they're going. They're all making a right at the end of the hallway I'm walking down, so I do the same. I start to look at the teachers' names on the slates outside the classroom doors. The hallway is crowded with kids moving in both directions. Someone bumps me and without thinking I shout, "Hey, watch it!" The boy stops and turns around, his face bright red. The hallway goes quiet for a moment and my face feels hot as I realize that I'm brand new and I just made myself sound like a real jerk, so I add, "Just kidding," with a half-smile. The boy rolls his eyes and turns to leave. The chatter in the hallway picks up again. Although I'm embarrassed that I called attention to myself before I was ready to, I feel a small surge of adrenaline and a jolt of happy energy. If that had turned into a fight, I would have won. I would have knocked that boy down, then taken his friends down too before getting to class and showing them why they'll soon start calling me The Answer Key.

Before I know it, I'm at the end of the hall and I haven't found Mr. Foster's room, so I turn around and walk back through the thinning crowd. People are finding their classrooms one by one and I feel my positive energy swiftly morph into a panicky sort of fear. My heart rate picks up as I start walking desperately from door to door. I still don't see Mr. Foster's name and I'm starting to look like I don't belong. I reach the other end of the hallway and begin to feel like a caged animal, now walking back in the original direction I'd taken. I look at my watch. One minute until the bell rings, so I break into a jog. This time when I reach the end of the hallway, I notice a staircase to my left. I take the stairs two by two, calling myself a different name with each wide step I take. "Loser, moron, worthless, stupid, jerk-face." I hit the top step, make a right out of the staircase, and see Mr. Foster's classroom right in front of me. I step across the threshold and slide into a seat in the front row just as the bell rings.

My heart is racing, sending adrenaline coursing through my veins. I try to slow my breathing and I notice my thoughts are racing too. My brain feels like the crowded hallway, jam-packed with thoughts moving in all directions, and I can barely hold on to one. Mr. Foster is a wiry middle-aged man with thick glasses and gray, thinning hair. He takes his place at the front of the classroom and begins to speak. He's saying something about getting started and about going around and introducing ourselves, and I realize to my horror that he will call on me first. I force myself to breathe. I try to remember my name as he points at me and motions for me to begin. I am silent and notice people beginning to whisper to one another. I clear my throat and suddenly feel my thoughts start to slow. My adrenaline surges in the right direction, carrying me like a massive wave, and words start flying from my mouth. "I'm Bob Krulish. I'm new here, from Long Island. I'm an A+ student, never missed a semester on the honor roll. Back home, they call me The Answer Key." I leave out the fact that I'm a golf star and I'll be on the team this year if the coach knows what's good for him. They'll just have to see for themselves. I finish by giving Mr. Foster a thumbs-up and he offers me a smile that feels condescending, but I don't care. The kids in my class look unimpressed, which I see as a challenge that I'm ready and willing to accept.

I make it through the first three periods without feeling any more surges of fear or panic. Science was a breeze and Spanish was a cakewalk. I coasted through English class and was the first to get an answer right about the book assigned for summer reading. Between classes, I was able to figure out that all the seventh-grade classrooms are in a single hallway in alphabetical order. Knowing that formula makes it easier to move from place to place and look like I know what I'm doing. I finally make it to Mrs. Porter's math class and slide into a front row seat, ready to show off the things I taught myself over the summer. There is a boy sitting next to me with round wire glasses and a face full of freckles. His hair is neatly combed and his black polo shirt is tucked into his khaki shorts. His backpack is sitting next to his desk on the floor and it's bursting with books and papers. He notices me looking at it, catches my eye, and says, "I know, I'm a packrat." He pauses as though he's sizing me up, then continues, "I'm George. You're Bob, right?"

"Yeah," I respond. "How do you know?"

"I'm in your homeroom. Answer Key? Brave thing to tell your class on the first day."

"I guess I'm just a brave guy," I say with a shrug and a smile.

Mrs. Porter steps out from behind her desk and takes her place at the front of the room. She is plump and jolly-looking, which is rare for math teachers—they're usually more severe. "Hello, class, and welcome!" she begins. "I'm happy to meet you all and look forward to jumping right into today's lesson, which is in geometry. Let's take a look at this shape we all know and love." She draws a triangle on the board.

SCORE! I think. The Pythagorean theorem.

I shoot my hand into the air.

"Yes? Mister…?" She points a chalky finger at me.

"Krulish. You're talking about the Pythagorean theorem, $a^2 + b^2 = c^2$."

Mrs. Porter raises an eyebrow. "That is correct Mr. Krulish and very impressive, but please, let's not skip ahead."

I feel a rush of happy energy wrap around my body and I smile knowing I can solve any problem she puts on the board before anyone else can even pick up a pencil. I look over at George, who glances at me and mouths the word "Nice."

Not only am I doing great, but I think I'm also about to make my first friend in the great state of New Mexico.

———

"Line up your shoulders," my dad's voice booms. I am standing at the tee set up in our backyard, getting ready to swing. Although I feel like my body is perfectly aligned, I wiggle my shoulders in response. My dad gives me the okay sign, even though I haven't actually moved an inch. I raise my driver and swing, sending the ball flying into the vacant lot behind our house. My dad lets out a "Heck yeah!" and adds, "See what happens when you listen to your old man?"

"Yeah," I respond as I shield my eyes, scanning the lot to see how far the ball travelled.

"If you don't make that team, I'm going down to the school myself to straighten those turkeys out."

I let out a small chuckle. I know that he wants me to make the golf team just so he can brag about it to the neighbors, his co-workers, and to anyone else who will listen, but I don't care. I let myself enjoy the attention for a moment before grabbing another ball from the bucket resting nearby on the lawn. I take the ball to the tee, set it up, and start to get into position. I know what I'm doing, but I still ask my dad, "How does this look?"

He stands back and eyes my position, walks over to me, moves my arms slightly, and jostles my body to adjust my stance. I now feel completely crooked, so I move right back to where I was as he walks six paces away. He stops, turns to face me, and after a moment says, "Perfect, let her rip." I wind up and whack the ball.

"Look at it fly!" he exclaims as I shield my eyes once more and watch the ball land in the vacant lot and roll several feet farther than the last one.

As my dad claps, he turns back toward me and gives me a thumbs-up. Then I notice him look past me and lock eyes on Rik and Kryse, who are sitting nearby on the grass. "Hey, Rik!" my dad calls out. "Why don't you get over here and hit a few with your brother?"

Rik blinks a few times before a wide smile spreads across his face. He hops up and breaks into a jog, leaving Kryse alone with her doll resting in her lap. Rik runs up to the bucket and picks out a ball, tosses it into the air and catches it before he walks to the tee, bends over, and balances the ball on it. My dad takes the driver from me, catches my eye, and raises his eyebrow before turning around and handing the club to Rik. My stomach flips.

"Here you go," my dad says, stepping back. "I'm not going to help you at all. I want to see what you can do on your own. I'm not even going to tell you that your stance looks like crap or that you need to straighten your arms. You just do your thing."

"Okay," Rik responds, lengthening his back and straightening his arms. Beads of sweat have formed on his forehead and are beginning to roll down his temples. The driver is a little too big for him, and he struggles to stand comfortably and remains visibly tense. He raises his arms behind him and I can see that they are crooked and that his legs are off-kilter. As he brings the club down toward the ball, he barely grazes the top of it, causing it to fall off the tee and roll hardly six feet in front of us. My dad begins to roar with laughter, instantly doubling over as if he can barely contain himself. I let myself smile even though I see that Rik's face is twisted into a grimace. He is fighting tears.

I reach for the bucket of balls and grab him another one so he can try again. I walk it to the tee and place the ball for him. I pat him on the shoulder, as if to say, "You got this," and step aside.

Just as my dad starts to catch his breath, Rik winds up to hit the ball and brings the driver down even harder than before. He misses the ball entirely this time, causing him to stumble with the force of his swing. My dad lets out a high-pitched guffaw as my brother tosses the club to the ground and walks quickly into the house. As he passes me, he coughs to cover his heaving breaths that I know will become full-blown sobs as soon as he slams the door behind him.

"He's no athlete," my dad says as he wipes his brow and composes himself. "He's no straight-A student either. Looks like it's up to you to carry on my legacy, Bobby."

Kryse is still sitting on the lawn with her doll, but now she's staring daggers at me as if I'm the one who manufactured this whole thing—as if I personally humiliated Rik in front of my dad and made him cry. I don't know what to say, so I grab a ball from the bucket, place it on the tee, grab the driver off the ground, square my shoulders, and hit the ball as hard as I can, sending it flying like a rocket ship into the great unknown.

〰〰〰

It's finally tryout day and I can't wait to blow everyone away. I'm standing in a row of boys dressed in khaki shorts and white polo shirts, as if dressing like they're on the team will help them perform. I'm the only one wearing a dark-colored shirt, which means I'll stick out in the coach's memory for more than just my legendary swing.

There is an empty tee between me and the next boy over until someone walks up, bends over, and places his ball. He stands up and stretches, and I look over to see that it's George, who locks eyes on me and smiles, revealing a mouth full of bright silver braces.

"Mr. Krulish, I presume?" he says, tipping his baseball hat.

"Hey George," I respond. "You play golf?"

"I do, kinda."

"What do you mean 'kinda'? You know you're at tryouts for the golf team, right?"

"Yes, I do, smart-aleck. I just do this because my mom makes me. She says I have to diversify if I want to get into Harvard one day."

We both laugh as the coach blows his whistle, signaling that it's time to start. One by one, each boy whacks a ball off their tees. Some sail far across the field; others fall short, rolling just a few feet in front of us. Everyone encourages each other, saying things like "You'll get 'em next time" and "Good try, man." I can't tell if the kindness is genuine or if it's meant to disarm, so I stay quiet and focused.

Soon, it is my turn. The moment I've been waiting for. I breathe in, feeling a rush of nerves, and breathe out, letting the fear go. I wind up and swing, hitting the ball perfectly, letting it fly so far across the field I can't see exactly where it lands. George looks impressed and I notice the coach make a note on his clipboard. I've nailed it, just like I'd planned. And now my dad can keep enjoying the glory of having me as his son, kicking everyone's behind and taking names.

Chapter 5

WATCHING HAPPY DAYS

T he road is so hot I can feel the warmth through my shoes as I walk. I imagine the asphalt sizzling and crackling, eating away at the rubber until it's so gooey I can barely lift my foot to take another step. The straps of my backpack dig into my shoulders, causing them to feel weak and tired beneath the weight of textbooks and notebooks I've brought home for the night. Tucked on top of the books, however, is something even more exciting. It's my first math test of the year and I got an A+ on it. I picture casually sliding it across the counter when my dad asks whether I got it back. I've been thinking about this moment all day.

Today was day twenty-two of school and so far, it's all happening exactly like I planned. I walked into school the new kid and in just a few weeks, I've shown everyone exactly what I'm made of. My teachers can't believe how far ahead I am. I wouldn't be surprised if I win every single academic award this year and bring home an average above a 4.0. Of course, I also made it onto the golf team and I know I will be named captain next week before our first meet. Even though technically, coach named Jonah Wilde captain, it won't be long before I take over the spot. Jonah is a bozo and my swing is way better than his. When I told my dad about it he was so happy, I thought he was going to hug me. Instead, he ran outside with a beer and his aerating spike and worked on the lawn until he spotted a neighbor he could share the news with.

Now, I am walking home with George, who, it turns out, lives just two blocks away. Once we figured that out, we started walking to and from school together every day. Now that we're both on the golf team, we do that together too, and on weekends we trade baseball cards, talk about golf, and even quiz one another when we need to study for tests.

When we get to my house, Rik and Kryse are already outside. They've tossed their backpacks by the mailbox and are riding in circles around the driveway. As I step onto the lawn, I give George a high five and say, "Later, man."

"See you tomorrow, sir!" he responds as he turns to head home.

I scamper across the lawn, bound up the two front steps and fling the front door open. The cold air conditioning blasts me in the face as the smell of meatballs and garlic fills my nose. I ease my shoes off one by one as the garage door swings open. My mom walks into the house, her hair tied back in a bandana. Her smock is covered in clay dust, her white sneakers splattered with speckles of paint. "Hey, son! How was school?" she asks, wiping her hands on her jeans.

"Good," I reply. "Dad home yet?"

"No, not yet," she says, glancing at her watch. "He should be here any minute." She takes off her smock and hangs it on a hook by the door, then walks toward the bathroom. "I'm going to freshen up. Go tell your brother and sister that it's almost dinnertime, will you?"

I open the door and shout, "Dinner!"

"I could have done that," Mom says. "Please just go outside and get them."

I roll my eyes and walk out the door toward Rik and Kryse and yell, "I said it's dinnertime! Mom says you've gotta get inside."

Rik swerves around in front of the lawn and pulls up in front of me with a screech. "Why don't you stop dipping in our Kool-Aid, Bobby?" he quips.

"Yeah!" Kryse pipes in, her pigtails flapping behind her in the breeze.

I breathe in to shout back but decide against it and instead turn back toward the house. I step off the sidewalk onto the short, stubby grass, my socks now soaked from the water that spilled from the sprinkler moments earlier. I get to the door, peel my socks off, and head straight to my backpack. I unzip the bag and pull out my test, admiring the A+ once more.

<hr />

It is pitch black outside and the world is silent. Well, except for the strange sounds of New Mexico wildlife that I'm still getting used to. On Long Island, our summer nights offered a concert of crickets and peeping frogs. Here, the crickets and night noises are softer, a low murmur accompanied by the buzz of insects circling the floodlights outside our house. Once in a while, there's a loud screech—sometimes it's a cat, other times it's a small animal falling prey to something bigger—a steady reminder that no matter where we live, the circle of life exists and we're all trapped in it. I crack my eye open to check the time. It's just past midnight and I haven't been able to sleep.

Once Rik and Kryse came in from outside this afternoon, we washed up and got ready for dinner. When we sat, Dad still wasn't home. Although my mom acted like things were just fine and offered several reasons he might not be here yet, I could tell she was worried. Even as she asked the usual questions about school, offered us seconds and thirds, and brought out scoops of Rocky Road ice cream for dessert, I noticed her voice quake one or twice. She tried to smile, but her eyes were sad as she checked her watch every few minutes and bounced her knee under the table.

Once we finished dinner, I sat at my desk to do my homework while Rik and Kryse did theirs in front of the TV, watching Happy Days. From my room, I could hear the sound of canned laughter, clanging pots and pans, and the hiss of running water. I tried to sink into my work and tune everything out, especially the rising fear that my dad's absence wasn't a good sign. Of course, I knew where he could be—where he likely was—but I also knew that things had been great recently. I couldn't imagine why he'd want to trade the peace we'd achieved for the chaos we'd escaped.

Now, in bed, I keep cycling through the formulas and equations I'd learned over the summer, picturing how I'd keep blowing my new math teacher away with everything I know. I stare at the clock, which glows 1:21 a.m. in bright red. 121, I think…the square root of 121 is 11. Answer Key strikes again.

I roll over, trying to get comfortable. My new bed is different than the one I'd slept in my entire life. I can feel the springs on my side, hard and unwelcoming, like they're just barely tolerating my existence. As I pull the blanket over my shoulder, I hear a familiar, soft sound coming from the hallway. I kick the blankets off my body and stand, making my way toward the door. I crack the door open and stick my head out to see my mom sitting on the floor with her back against the wall. She is outside of the bedroom she shares with my dad. The phone is by her side, the cord coiled neatly like a sleeping snake. My mom's knees are pulled into her chest, her slippers set aside, her bare feet touching the ground. Her head is against her knees, her dark curly hair spilling over her shins. Not yet used to the new house and its quirks, I step on a floorboard that creaks loudly, and my mom looks up. She locks eyes on me and looks hopeful for a moment. Her smile drops as soon as she realizes it's me.

"Oh goodness," she says, wiping her eyes. "Why do you always do that?"

"Sorry, I heard something out here, I wasn't sure what it was. Are you okay?"

"This isn't for you to worry about," she says. "Want to sit down with me for a minute?" She pats the floor next to her.

I walk over and take my place on the floor, my arm touching hers. She rests her head on my shoulder. I feel a tear drop from her eyelid onto my bicep and roll down my arm. I don't touch it out of fear that it'll embarrass her if she thinks I've noticed. She takes a deep breath and I smell cigarettes on her as she exhales.

"Your dad still isn't home," she says with a sniffle. "I don't know where he is."

"I know," I sigh and continue, "I'm sorry, Mom."

"I'm sorry too. I don't know what I did wrong," she says, her head still on my shoulder.

I reach over with my free hand and rub the top of her head. It seems strange to comfort her in this way, but I try to ignore how awkward I feel. Instead, I am flooded with sadness and fear. I know the good stuff probably wouldn't have lasted forever, but I wish I could count on just a few more nights of calm before things go back to the way they used to be. I wonder if there is any hope that this is all a misunderstanding or a mistake. I picture my dad in a fiery car crash, being loaded into an ambulance, and later resting on a bed unconscious, just feet away from a phone. I shake the image in favor of logic, which is only slightly more comforting.

"Maybe he had to work?" I suggest. "Or maybe…y'know …he had a mission?"

She picks her head up off my shoulder, turns toward me, and holds my gaze, tears spilling over her bottom lids. We both know it's crazy to think he's doing anything other than reconnecting with Maureen. But she nods her head anyway and says, "Maybe."

It is morning and I didn't sleep for more than an hour last night. My dad never came home. I spent the night tense and angry, tossing and turning, my jaw clenched. I wasn't just angry for myself, but for my mom, who I know fully believed we had defeated the demons that had threatened to pull our family apart at the seams. I am sitting at the kitchen table watching her crack eggs into a bowl. She is staring straight ahead, her hair rumpled at the back, her apron tied loosely around her housecoat. Her relaxed, sunny demeanor and easy smile are all gone, replaced with heavy, thick disappointment. The phone never rang last night, nor did it ring this morning, so I know she never received an explanation from my dad. Yet, this time, my mom seems to be letting the silence speak for itself. She isn't pretending that things are okay or that there's a chance he was working—she's letting herself sit in it. The honesty of it all feels better than I thought it would, but the anxiety about my dad's return feels worse than ever. I am looking over my homework, with a pile of textbooks next to me that are resting next to a stack of papers with my algebra test on top. If he does come home, I want to be ready to ease the tension by sliding the test his way.

Rik and Kryse seem unfazed by my dad's absence. My mom places sweating glasses of orange juice in front of each of us as Rik scrambles to finish his homework. I peek over his shoulder and notice that many of his answers are wrong. I open my mouth to tell him but decide to leave it alone. Nothing I say will change the fact that he doesn't care to try, and I don't want him to think I'm just another person judging him so I choose to keep it to myself.

Just as my mom reaches for a plate in the cabinet, the front door bangs open. My mom drops the dish, which hits the floor and shatters. She pivots and walks with purpose toward the front of the house. She shouts, "Where the heck were you?"

Rik and Kryse gather their papers, grab their backpacks, and scurry out through the back door. The weeks of peace in the house haven't numbed their instinct to flee. I, on the other hand, am frozen. Everything inside me is screaming at me to run, but my body isn't moving. I am still clutching my pencil when my dad shouts back, "That's none of your business."

They've stopped outside the kitchen door. My mom is pressed against the doorframe, my dad in front of her. "It is my business, Bob," she cries out. "This is our life."

"Oh, really? Well, who puts this roof over our heads? Who puts food on our table?"

"You do," she responds in a measured tone.

"That's right. I do. You don't own me. You don't own my time. I do what I want, when I want. Understood?"

Though I can't see them, I can feel him inching closer to her. He is breathing hard. My mom is silent.

"Do. You. Under-stand?" he asks again, over pronouncing each syllable.

"I…" she whispers.

"You nothing!" he shouts, driving his fist into the wall. I am so startled I nearly jump out of my seat. My chair scratches the tile loudly as I scoot back, alerting my dad to my presence. He crashes around the corner. His eyes are wild, though his hair is neatly combed, parted at the side like it always is. The smell of his aftershave hits my nose as he leans over the table, points a rigid finger at me, and says, "What the heck are you doing sitting here like an idiot? What, are you spying on us?"

"I was just about to go to school," I say, my throat tight.

"What, was Mommy making you breakfast?" he says in a high-pitched, mocking tone.

My mom comes around the corner wiping her face. She walks to the stove, looks at me, and says, "Scrambled eggs today?"

"I'm just gonna get going," I say, beginning to gather my things.

"You better get going. And you," he says to my mom, through clenched teeth. "If you think we're done talking about this, you're dead wrong." He slams his hand on the table, sending my orange juice flying. It splatters all over my textbooks and spills on the pile of papers right next to them. Noticing his mistake, without missing a beat, he swipes his hand across the table, sending the books, the papers, and the cup crashing to the floor.

Without a word, I bend down to pick it all up. My dad tosses me a rag, though I don't bother wiping anything down. I just pile my wet, sticky school things, grab my jacket, and run past my mom out the back door.

I stand in the yard for a moment to catch my breath. I am out of practice after a summer of relative calm, and the adrenaline rush feels extreme. I hear my mom's voice. It is loud and shaky and I can't make out what she's saying. Then I hear my dad's thundering voice shout over hers and he's saying words like disrespectful, witch, and tramp. I duck down so they won't see me run past the window behind the sink. I cut down the driveway and onto the sidewalk. I know my dad will come stomping out of the house any moment with his briefcase in hand, then he'll jump into his car and fly down the street. I pray I can get to school before he drives past me.

I see George in the distance but pretend like I don't and pick up the pace. I don't want to make up an excuse or laugh about the mess; I just want to disappear into thin air. I look down and realize I'm holding the sticky pile of books and papers against my chest, which has made my clothes damp. I stop for a moment, bend down, and place the pile on the ground as I unzip my backpack. As I do, I notice a pink stain on my shirt. I look at the paper on top of the stack and realize the red ink my A+ was written in is wet and running off the paper, disappearing into the ether with the last of the sweet summer smiles we shared under the bright desert sun.

Chapter 6

DAD

I am standing outside the house trying to force myself to go in. Staring at it from the street, it looks normal enough. The lawn is pillowy and plush thanks to my dad's obsessive aeration and the sprinkler that he runs all day, the hedges are trimmed, and the paint is crisp and white. But after this morning, I know the inside of our home is filled with things that are far less pretty. I know my family—I know my dad—and I know this summer was an anomaly.

I've gone to church with my family on and off over the years, and I know that we're supposed to believe that miracles happen. We're supposed to pray and know that God loves us and that he'll care for us and keep bad things from happening. Sometimes I think my family is exempt from all that, because my dad's way of being is so powerful, it renders God totally helpless. When my dad is at his worst, he seems bent on ruining every-thing with the fury of a tornado, a hurricane, and a tsunami combined.

I finally force myself to walk across the lawn, up the front stairs, and turn the doorknob. When I push the door, it hits something solid, so I shove it open with all the strength I can muster. As I step inside, I see our moving boxes have been reassembled. Some have already been packed, others are half-full, and the rest are empty and seem ready to receive. The house is silent and devoid of cooking smells, though I smell cigarette smoke and sense palpable tension. My backpack still hanging from my shoulders, I walk toward the kitchen to see my mom standing outside, dressed exactly as she was when I left this morning. She has stretched the cord from the kitchen phone all the way outside and is pacing close to the house, tethered by the strained pink wire. She notices me and quickly puts out her cigarette, then motions that she'll be inside in a minute.

I inhale sharply, letting the reality set in. We have to be moving and the only thing I can think is that we've got to be going home to Long Island. As much as I've loved getting into a new school and building my reputation from scratch, going home would be truly awesome. I would get to hang out with my old friends again; I'd get onto the golf team, no problem; and I'd wow everyone with my stories about living in the desert and dominating the school like the pro that I am. I picture myself strolling up to my old school, pants still dusty, skin still tan from my summer adventure, and giving all my friends high fives as I walk through the door, now king of the school just because I came back. I am startled out of my fantasy by my mom saying, "Sorry, that was Nanny. How was school?"

"How was school?" I respond. "How about just cutting to the chase? Are we moving back home?" I'm startled by my own tone and feel badly for a second. My mom needs my kindness now more than ever, but I don't apologize.

As she inhales deeply, I notice a bruise beneath her left eye, "Not exactly. We're going to Florida to be with Nanny and Poppa. We leave tomorrow."

"Florida?" I manage. I am so shocked I can barely speak.

"Yes," she responds.

"But what about school? What about golf?" My voice begins to crack as I continue, "And my friends? I like it here."

"I don't know what to tell you, you've got to forget about it. You'll go to a new school as soon as we get settled. You'll make new friends. Your father's found a new job. We've got to go."

I want to ask her why. I want to scream at the top of my lungs. I want to tell her how hard I've been trying and how hard I worked and how much progress I made and how George was becoming a best friend and how I was about to knock Jonah out of the top spot and become captain of the golf team and that I didn't want to go. I want to punch the walls and scream and kick, but instead, I nod my head and leave the kitchen. I'm not like my dad, I can control myself. I can lock the anger up. So I grab a box and walk down the long hallway to my room and start packing up my stupid life once again.

———

Everything about this move is different. There is no sense of cautious optimism. There are no smiles, no laughter, no singing. Beloved items aren't placed carefully in boxes. This time, things are tossed like trash, swept off of surfaces, thrown into boxes and bags. Things feel rushed, as if we're racing the clock, waiting for a bomb to detonate.

My dad is stomping through the house, kicking shoes out of the way, muttering curse words under his breath. He has remained in a state of rage since his fight with my mom, which is unusual. Usually, once a fight tapers off, there is at least some kind of an ending to the ordeal. He makes excuses, tries to justify his actions, then expects everyone to get over it. Today, though, he's continuing to let things boil, as if the rage won't stop until the family evaporates before his very eyes.

Rik and Kryse seem okay with what's going on. Rik hadn't settled in yet and although he did make a few friends in the neighborhood, there is nothing here that makes him want to stay. Kryse is still young enough that my mom could talk to her about making even more new friends and get her excited about leaving. Plus, she knows that living near Nanny and Poppa means treats and presents almost every day, which seems way better to her than a boring life in the desert.

I, on the other hand, am not okay. I'm not okay because I know that my dad caused this. Even if I don't know exactly what's happening, I know for a fact that he's moving us once again because it's best for him and no one else.

I've worked so hard in the past few weeks to set myself up to rule my school in Albuquerque and now I'll have to do it all again in a whole new place. Every part of me feels exhausted and defeated. I just want to run away.

I hear a car pull up in front of the house and I peek through the blinds in my bedroom. It's my aunt and uncle. Clearly, they've heard the news and want to offer help and say goodbye. I know my dad won't like this because it means my mom has been "gossiping," so I wait to hear him explode. Then, it comes. "Get the heck off my lawn!" he bellows, and my aunt and uncle walk backward as if someone cast a spell to send them moving in reverse. They are yelling back at him but he just keeps repeating "GOODBYE!" until their engine revs and they leave. I wonder when I will see them again and decide that it doesn't matter anyway.

I walk across the hall into the bathroom and close the door, clicking the lock behind me. I turn on the water to muffle the sound and whisper-scream as many curse words as I can think of, then look myself in the eye. I look awful. Tired, angry, burdened, and I feel like I could explode. Then I notice the pink stain on my shirt and remember the ink running off my math test. I wish that I could punch my dad square in the jaw.

〜〜〜

It is 10 p.m. and we're in the car, hurtling down the highway. My dad has been driving close to ninety miles per hour as if he can't wait to get us to Florida. He claims he has an important job there with a moving company and that we need to get there fast, but I don't believe anything he says anymore and my mom has barely spoken a word. She's no longer smiling even a little bit, nor is she telling us that we'll be okay and that we'll love our new home and that we'll be happier near Nanny and Poppa. She's surrendered to the new vision Dad has for our life, and it doesn't seem to matter to her what that looks like. She isn't trying to hide her black eye, which looks deeper and more pronounced by the hour. She hasn't brushed her hair or put on her lipstick—instead she's stayed in her housecoat and slippers, and now she's staring out the window into the darkness.

My mom wanted to wait until morning to leave, but my dad started throwing stuff into the trunk as soon as my aunt and uncle peeled out of the driveway. He had made his decision about where we were going and he wasn't going to sit around and wait. I quickly packed a bag, then walked out of the house, planning to go tell George that we were leaving. Before I could even step off the property, my dad called me over to the car and barked orders at me. He wanted me to get my bag from my room and have my brother and sister pack theirs, then put them in the car immediately. Once I did that, he had me turn off the water to the house, unplug all the lamps, and lock the windows, and before I knew it, it was dark and he was forcing us into the car before I could get to George's to say goodbye. When I asked about the rest of our things, my dad muttered something about putting everything in storage before slamming his foot on the gas so hard that our bodies lurched. Now, I am holding a notebook open to a blank page and a pencil trying to decide what to tell George. I strain to see in the pitch black but catch a stretch of pulsating light from a row of lights along the highway and start,

Dear George,

My family and I had to leave because my dad is crazy.

I erase it and start again…

Dear George,

My family and I had to leave because my grandparents bought a mansion in Florida and they want us to move in. I was asked to be captain of their local golf team and they wanted me there right away because they have a match this weekend. Sorry I didn't get to say good-bye. I'll write more soon.

Sincerely,

Mr. Krulish

I fold the letter and put it in my backpack, promising myself that I'll send it from the first motel we stop at. But my dad shows no signs of stopping. The radio is on and he is drumming on the steering wheel, chewing sunflower seeds and periodically taking swigs of Fresca. My mom's eyes are closed now and Rik and Kryse have been asleep for at least an hour. The car is illuminated for a moment in the glare of a passing light, and my dad catches my eye in the rearview mirror.

"You look pissed off, Bobby."

I don't know how to respond, so I say nothing but continue to look at him in the mirror.

"Listen, son." He's trying to make his voice sound soft, but it doesn't work. He sounds harsh, like he's already on the defensive. He continues, "You might not get it now, but one day, you'll understand where I'm coming from. You've got to follow the work. When an opportunity comes up, you grab it. You pick your things up and you go. Will that piss people off? Sure. But when you know you're right, you know you're right."

"Okay," I respond. Suddenly, I remember my golf clubs still sitting in the garage. My fists clench into tight balls.

"Yeah," he responds. "It is okay." He sips his Fresca and starts drumming on the steering wheel, before cracking the window and spitting a wad of chewed seeds into the cool night.

The sun is peeking up from beneath the horizon and we've only stopped once for gas. The rest of the family slept while my dad fiddled with the pump, kicking the tire in frustration when he couldn't get the gas cap off. When he stormed inside to pay, I jumped out of the car and snuck over to a bush to pee, keeping my eye on him the entire time. I knew there would be trouble if he caught me out of the car, so I went as fast as I could. I saw him turn to leave and was relieved to see him pause and look at something on the shelf. It gave me just enough time to get back into the car and pretend to be asleep, my head resting on the door and the metal lock jammed into my temple.

Now, as the sun rises, I notice that the traffic is getting heavier. My stomach rumbles and I hope my mom wakes soon and offers a snack or suggests that we stop. My dad is weaving between the cars around us, still maintaining high speed. I see brake lights in front of us and squeeze my eyes shut, bracing for impact. My dad swerves just in time, muttering curse words and pounding the dashboard. The rest of the family is awake now and we're jostled back and forth with every turn of the wheel. It feels like we are on a speeding train that could derail at any moment. Traffic picks up even more, which tells me we must be nearing a major city—Dallas, I think—and my dad no longer seems to care about safety of any kind. Rik and Kryse are screaming; my mom is holding on to the door, trying to keep herself from sliding into my dad. I notice Rik and Kryse had taken off their seat belts to sleep more comfortably, so I scramble to help them get buckled in before fastening my own seat belt as tightly as I can.

"Get outta my way!" my dad screams. "Learn to drive!" He rolls down the window and the wind rips and roars through the car as he continues to yell. "What the heck are you doing, you motherless pig!?"

Up ahead cars have slammed on their brakes. "Dad!" I yell, instinctively grabbing onto Kryse's arm.

He slams his foot on the brakes, sending our bodies hurling forward, the seat belts straining to hold us in place. The car stops, barely an inch behind the car in front of us.

My mom turns around to make sure we are okay. As she leans over the front seat to help us get readjusted, my dad starts to laugh. First, it's a quiet chuckle, then it spills from his body, high-pitched, almost hysterical. My mom sinks back into her seat and he bats at her shoulder, then looks around and realizes the rest of us are silent. "Oh, come on, everybody. Lighten up!" He laughs for another moment, catches his breath, and says, "Who wants pancakes?"

The remaining fifteen hours of the drive were just as bad. We never stopped to sleep, just grabbed naps when we hit stretches of open road. My dad's mood has stayed unpredictable since he crashed into the house yesterday morning. It's hard to believe that only yesterday I was sitting at the breakfast table holding my first test of the year. I also can't believe I was stupid enough to think that showing my dad the test might make any difference at all. Nothing anyone does can calm my dad when he's like this—it just has to wear off in time.

We pulled up in front of Nanny and Poppa's house after darkness had already fallen. The air was soupy and wet, the exact opposite of the chilly nighttime desert air I had come to love. Although it was late, Nanny and Poppa came to the door and wrapped us in warm hugs. Their house smelled the same as ever, like lemon-fresh cleaner and mothballs. Resting on the kitchen table was a plate of fresh cookies. Rik, Kryse, and I each grabbed several and quickly began crunching into them. Our mom watched, expressionless, as Nanny laughed and said, "Wow, you've got some hungry kids!" She couldn't know that a pancake break-fast, which ended with my dad throwing a pile of change on the table and storming outside because his pancakes tasted "like dog crap," was the only real meal we'd had in a full day.

Now, Nanny is handing out blankets and pillows and is telling each of us where we can sleep. My dad is already snoring on the plastic-cov-ered sofa and we tiptoe around him. I get to sleep on the pullout couch in the den, which was my favorite room in their house. I am finally alone after what feels like a lifetime and the silence is so soft and comforting, I feel like I'm in a cocoon. I'm still wearing my shirt with the ink smudge on it, my golf shorts, and sneakers, but I am too tired to change and I wouldn't know where to find nightclothes if I wanted them. I kick my shoes off, wrap the itchy crochet blanket around my body, and curl into a fetal position on the pullout bed. My ears are ringing as I drift off to sleep, my body still convinced that it's in motion. I sink into a dream where I'm back in the car, watching through the windshield as we hurtle toward a car that has stopped in front of us. My dad is laughing hard and takes his hands off the wheel. I wake with a start just as our car careens into oncoming traffic.

Chapter 7

BAGGING GROCERIES

The bruise underneath my mom's eye has faded, but now it's replaced with heavy bags that reveal how little rest she's getting. She's been trying to act like things are okay and like we're just finding our new routine, but I can tell that what's happened has broken her. Everything she does feels forced, like she's acting out life as it should be, but her performance lacks heart, as if she's playing a role she no longer wants.

The morning after we arrived at Nanny and Poppa's house, we woke up and my dad was nowhere to be found. He'd unpacked his trunk and left while we were still sleeping, leaving its contents in the driveway. At first we wondered if he'd gone out for the paper or maybe to get doughnuts, which he sometimes did when he was sorry, or we wondered if he'd gone in to start his new job. But as day turned to night, it became clear that something wasn't right. Although my mom seemed sad, I felt some relief. She was being taken care of by her parents for the moment and the threat of my dad's explosive temper was gone, as if it had receded back into the darkness and dragged him with it.

Now it's been a few days with no word at all. Nanny and Poppa helped us get set up in a rental house just down the street from them. They brought over extra furniture from their house and some stuff donated by friends of theirs, set up the rooms, and filled the fridge with fresh orange juice and lemonade, with meatballs and cutlets.

My dad has been gone for more than a week now and everything inside me says he's gone for good, but my mom just can't accept it. She is acting as though he left to do an errand, then tried to get home but lost his way. At night she lies on the couch in the living room with the lights off, the TV casting a pulsating glow. The phone rests on the coffee table, just inches from her head. Now I'm heating food my grandparents brought over, meat loaf and mashed potatoes, and I'm plating it before calling everyone to the table. I know we'll sit in silence, but it doesn't matter. Sitting for dinner is the only thing we still do that feels remotely normal. I place the last piece of meat loaf on my plate and give myself an extra serving of potatoes.

"Dinner!" I yell.

My mom comes walking into the kitchen, Rik and Kryse not far behind. We all sit and my mom eyes my plate, noticing the big portion. Then her eyes drift to the empty chair. "Well," she says, "I guess if your father comes home, there are still meatballs in the fridge."

I nod and add, "And there is some spaghetti in there too," and smile at her, although I know there's no point in thinking about his return.

Rik and Kryse eat quickly and excuse themselves. They run into the living room and flip the TV to Fat Albert, leaving me alone at the table with Mom. She sniffs and says, "I'm sorry about your friends. I know you were really finding your way in Albuquerque."

My throat feels tight, but I respond, "Thanks. Yeah, I was."

"I hate that we had to leave. I thought things had really changed," she says, pushing food around with her fork.

"I do too." I look at her sad eyes and continue, "Hey, I never told you. I got an A+ on my first test of the year."

For the first time since New Mexico, her eyes look happy for a moment and her lips curl into a half smile. "I am so proud of you," she says, reaching out to put her hand on mine. In that moment, I can see my mom through the fog of grief and I know she's still in there.

"Thanks," I say, wiping my mouth. "Do you want to play cards or something tonight?"

"Well, maybe later. I still want us to get out tonight."

The color drains from my face. It's the last thing I want to do, but I know my mom is serious and won't be able to sit still unless I agree. I nod my head and start to clear the dishes while she grabs her coat and drapes it over her shoulders. As soon as the dishes are in the sink, I get my jacket from my room, put it on, grab a flashlight, and walk into the living room. "Guys," I say to Rik and Kryse, "Mom and I are going out for a little bit. Just watch TV and don't do anything stupid, okay?"

"Us do anything stupid," Rik says. "You're the one doing something stupid. You're not going to find him."

I look over my shoulder to make sure Mom isn't nearby, then turn back and say, "You think I don't know that? But I have to go. Mom needs this."

"Whatever," Rik says, turning back to the TV before adding, "Have fun."

I walk to the door and step outside, surprised to find my mom already in the car, smoking a cigarette. Since my dad took the Lincoln, we've been borrowing my grandparents' old Chevy Bel Air, which feels like a tin can. I open the door, my mom turns the key and begins backing out of the driveway before I can close it. "I hope they don't kill each other," she says.

"They won't, I talked to them."

"Thanks," she says, placing a hand on my shoulder.

She makes a left at the end of our street and drives slowly down the main road into town. She slows the car to a crawl every so often, gesturing to different buildings and houses where she wants me to shine the flashlight. Every time, I strain my eyes as if I'm looking hard for my dad—searching the structure and its property for signs of life. Sometimes we'll spot a parked black Lincoln and she'll check the license plate. When it doesn't match my dad's she'll ask me to get out and peek through the windows, just to make sure it isn't his.

After an hour of looking, my mom turns the car back toward our house and we continue the drive in silence. I shine my flashlight through the window once in a while, squinting as though I might see something. She slows the car and waits for my signal before crawling to a start again. Finally, we arrive back at the house, and she reaches her hand out to stop me as I move to get out. "Listen, I want to say thank you for coming out to look for your dad with me every night."

"You don't have to thank me."

"Well, I feel like I should." She shifts her body as though she's uncomfortable and continues, "I think it's time that you and I consider getting jobs. I can't ask Nanny and Poppa to support us for much longer."

"What about school?"

"I'll make the call and get you kids into school first thing tomorrow, but you and I need to figure out a way to bring some money into this house."

My throat tightened and my stomach flipped. I felt a rush of adrenaline shoot through my veins. My heart rate picked up and my breathing quickened. Although I knew things would change with my dad being gone, I never imagined that I'd have to fill his shoes this way. Suddenly, dreams of being on the golf team and making new friends seemed out of reach, fantasies that I was watching fade before my eyes and vanish into thin air. I could feel my brows furrow and my jaw tense, so I tried to relax my face before my mom noticed. "Let's just go in," I said, opening the door.

"Okay," she replied. "Let's get the kids to bed and figure out a plan."

I took a deep breath and walked toward the house with the weight of the world on my shoulders.

~~~

The beeping sound of the cash register will eventually drive me crazy. I'm so certain of it sometimes I picture myself in a straitjacket in a room with padded walls, rocking back and forth whispering "Beep," over and over and over. I am getting really great at bagging groceries, so great that there are several customers who will only get into line at the register where I'm working. I start with the heavy, solid stuff, like boxes and cans. I put them at the bottom, then place softer things on top, like bread, fruit, and eggs. I keep cold stuff, like meat and cheese, together in a separate bag; that way customers can go right to their refrigerator with the cold bag and to the pantry with the others. So far, it seems like I'm the best employee the store has ever seen. It can't hurt that I come to work with my mom every day, so I'm never even a second late.

Today, I'm moving quickly, like a well-oiled machine. I've been getting a good amount of rest at night and have gotten back to studying the things I know will put me ahead of the kids in my new school. Sometimes I think about George and the letter in my backpack, which I sent from Nanny and Poppa's as soon as we arrived. I imagine him reading it and feeling impressed, but wonder if he feels sad when he walks past our old house on his way to school.

Since we got our jobs, I've noticed Mom slowly coming back to life, now only asking me to come with her to look for my dad once in a while. Now that we have money coming in and discounted food from the store, she is finally cooking again. I feel nostalgic for the days when I'd come home from a day at school and spread my papers on my desk and dive into schoolwork. I'm trying not to think about what it'll be like when we start school next week and I'm writing papers and studying for tests before and after shifts at the store. I know we can't afford for me to miss a shift and when I think about that fact my throat feels tight, like someone is standing behind me with their hands around my neck.

I try to shake the feeling by reviewing formulas, but then a head of cauliflower rolls toward me, and I feel my thoughts lock onto it. I think about the word cauliflower and how it starts with a c. Then, my mind latches onto the letter c and I begin reciting as many words as I can in my head that begin with it.

Cauliflower, cat, Christmas, cake, coffee, cradle, crib, cancer, coffin.

I laugh at myself for playing a word association game alone in my head but realize that for a moment it actually distracted me. So, I do it again with the next item, a loaf of bread.

Bread, bird, boat, blue, blue jeans, blast, blaze, blitz, balloon, baboon.

My brain continues with every item that rolls my way and soon I'm handing the bags to the customer and wishing her a good afternoon. There is a break for a moment and I look across the store to the deli counter and see my mom slicing turkey for a woman wearing cutoff shorts over a bathing suit and a visor that says Boca Raton. My mom is working methodically, her hair tucked into a hairnet, her pristine white coat buttoned up to the very top. The woman is tapping her foot impatiently while watching my mom slice the meat and pile it onto a scale. She catches my mom's eye and motions for her to hurry up. I am instantly filled with rage. Without thinking I shout, "Hey!" and she turns her head sharply to look at me. My mom lifts her head and locks eyes on me, her eyes wide with surprise. Suddenly aware of what I've done, I drop my shoulders and cough loudly, trying to pretend they were mistaken and I was just clearing my throat. My mom goes back to slicing the turkey and the woman turns back around, then begins to drum her long pink fingernails on the counter. I look back at the register just as more items start sliding toward me. I get out a bag and grab for a box of Apple Jacks and start listing every A word that comes to mind.

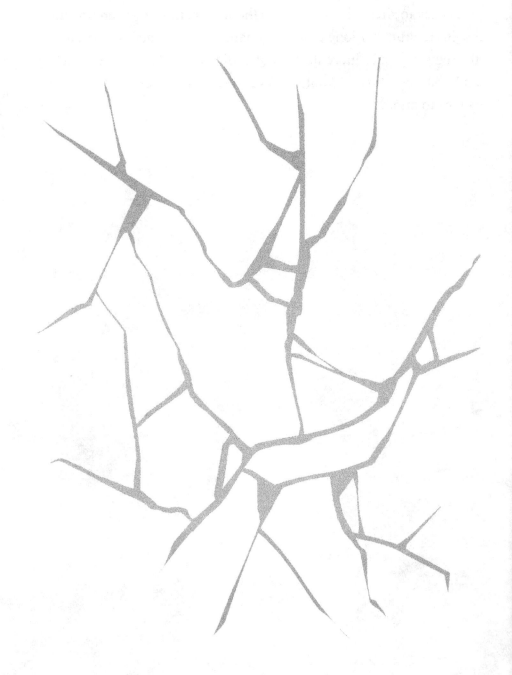

PART
II

Chapter 8

"SENATOR KRULISH SLASHES FUNDING"

The noise is thunderous. It rips through my chest, rattling my ribs. The jet hurtles down the runway, my frame seemingly glued to the seat as I pull back on the yoke and take to the sky. The plane climbs up, up, up, slicing through clouds. I am weightless now. I bank the plane left, then right. My stomach flips as I ease the plane into a roll—one, then two, then three. I imagine what this looks like from the ground—how cool it must be to see the plane doing such skilled acrobatics. I am playing in the sky like a god.

Beep, beep, beep, beep, beep, beep, beep.

Just as I finish my final roll, I right the plane and scan the instrument panel only to see every light flashing. There is a problem with both engines and, somehow, I'm dangerously low on fuel. My mind races to make the right calculations, trying to figure out whether I can make it back to base. The beeping continues, cutting through the deep, thick roar of the engines, making it impossible for me to think.

Instinctively, I reach out and start punching at the panel, but I'm not making contact.

I am falling.

As I hit the ground, my eyes burst open and I am breathing hard. It takes a moment before reality sets in. I'm in my dorm room on the cold linoleum floor. I am dripping with sweat and my nose is bleeding. My roommate's bed is made. He is gone already, so it's just Robert Plant staring at me from a poster on the wall as I peel myself off the floor. I grab a wad of tissues and dab at the blood collecting on my upper lip. There is no pain, only lingering exhilaration.

Once the bleeding stops, I toss the ball of tissues in the trash and start prepping for the day. I pull a shirt over my head and step into a pair of jeans before sliding my feet into sandals and grabbing my toothbrush and toothpaste. I open the door and let it slam behind me as I make my way to the communal bathroom. The smell of Aqua Net, Old Spice, and cigarette smoke hangs in the air I as walk past room after room with their doors propped open. Many are filled with furniture haphazardly built by overzealous dads and fluffy quilts and plastic bins bought by overbearing moms. I walk into the bathroom and head to the sink to brush my teeth and splash water on my face before checking my watch, only to realize that I'm running behind. I know Donna will be waiting for me outside the dorm, so I finish quickly, run back into the hallway and to my room, which is bare compared to the others. I head to my desk, sweep a pile of papers into my backpack, then walk out, leaving my like-new schoolbooks behind.

I lock the door behind me, run down the stairs, and push the outside door open. Donna is there, leaning against the wall, her bright, blond hair glistening in the morning sunlight. She waves to me and smiles, her face relaxed and joyful, and I run to her and wrap her in a bear hug before taking her hand and beginning our walk across campus.

"Sleep well?" she asks, her voice chipper.

"Yeah, I had awesome dreams," I said. "Can't wait for the program to start."

"I know you can't," she replied. "If I'm honest, though, I think I'll worry about you when you fly those things."

"You don't have to worry about me," I scoff.

"Yeah, I know. I really do," she says, raising my hand to her mouth and kissing it.

"Besides, sure, the fighter pilot program is going to be awesome, but it's not forever. You know I'll be safe behind a desk where I belong soon enough."

"Only you," she says with a laugh.

"Only me what?"

"Only you make your way into the most competitive program at school just for fun."

"That's why you love me!" I say, draping my arm over her shoulders and pulling her close.

We walk for another few minutes in silence, waving to friends as they hurry past. A heavy, warm breeze ruffles our hair and I look over at Donna just as she tucks a loose strand behind her ear and her diamond earring twinkles in the light. I feel a rush of butterflies. For a moment, I imagine our future. We're playing in the bright green yard in front of our massive house with our five kids—a big game of tag all together. Surrounded by a white picket fence and fireflies, we run, breathless. My tie is loose, I'm relaxed, and everyone is happy. I can see it so clearly; it makes me feel like jumping into the air and punching the sky. Instead, I pull her close, kiss her on the cheek, and say, "I love you so much."

"No, I love you so much," she says with a giggle.

We arrive at the building where the student government offices are and I give Donna one last kiss and say, "I'll see you later, okay?"

"Yes, good luck today," she responds. "And don't forget about dinner with my parents tonight. Pick me up at six?"

"Sure," I say with a smile and push through the doors of the old, brick building.

As soon as I enter, I notice a guy walking toward me. He glares at me and says nothing, though his big brown eyes narrow as they burrow into me. I recognize him, but I can't think where from. My brain starts flipping through names and faces like it's sorting through a card catalog of all the people I've ever met or interacted with, yet I'm coming up blank. He brushes past me and mutters, "Jerk," before striding quickly to the door and pushing it hard.

He stomps out of the building, and suddenly, I remember him. Jasper O'Hara, head of the school's marching band, which I'd recently defunded by 50 percent. I relax. This is exactly why people like Jasper aren't as successful as people like me. If he'd stop wasting time holding a grudge and start thinking about fundraisers, their problems would be solved. Car wash, bake sale, walkathon. There, I thought of three ways to raise money in less than ten seconds. Who's the jerk now?

I grab a school newspaper from the rack in the hallway and walk into the student government office with purpose. I know I have more budgets to review today before my physical, then dinner with Donna's parents. The physical is the very last step I have before I'm officially accepted into the fighter pilot training program. It's just a formality, though. After my meetings with Captain Baker, the head of the program, there is no doubt about my acceptance status. When I heard about the program, I didn't just apply. I set up a private meeting with Captain Baker in his office and, over a cigar and black coffee, told him all about my stellar history with various golf leagues, my perfect streak of grades, and my future as a US senator. He couldn't wait to get me into the program after that. When I left, I swear I could smell the deep, toxic tang of jet fuel.

I walk into the office, grab a disposable cup, and slosh coffee into it with my free hand. Then I head to my desk, tossing the paper onto it first before sitting down in my chair. I put my bag on the floor, open the flap, and dig until I find my pipe, which I pull out and stuff with loose tobacco from my desk drawer, then I light it. I feel like Pablo Escobar taking long, pensive puffs of the sweet smoke. I linger in the moment, taking a few more drags before leaning forward to grab the pile of manila folders that contain each of the school clubs' proposed budgets. I prop my feet on the desk and lean back, opening the folder on my lap. I start with Spanish club and barely read three sentences before I decide to defund it completely. Why on earth would Spanish club need a budget? Speaking Spanish is free. I pull a red pen from my pocket and put a big x at the top of the paper and shove it back into the folder. I feel a jolt of pride as I picture how much money I've just saved the student government. Our account has never been this full.

I reach for the next folder when something on the front page of the school newspaper catches my eye. It's my name, right at the very top. I pull the paper toward me, unfold it, and read the headline, which says, "Student Senator Krulish Slashes Funding." I scan the article, picking out words and phrases like bullying, unsupportive, and lacking real school spirit. I laugh to myself, then notice a quote from the student council president, James, who says, "We are aware of the situation. It's something we're working to fix." I can hardly believe what I'm reading. They're "working to fix" the awesome things I'm doing? They should be kissing my feet! Then, it dawns on me that I saw James yesterday. He knew this article was coming out; he knew it would make me look awful in front of everyone, especially Donna. Yet, he didn't have the guts to tell me about it? I feel my face flush with anger.

Suddenly, James strides into the office without looking at me and sits down in his chair.

"What the heck is this?" I say, standing up and pushing my chair out of the way.

"Good morning to you too, Bob," he replies.

I come around my desk and walk quickly toward him, then slap the paper down on his desk and say, "You knew about this?"

"You're so intense, man," he says, rolling his eyes.

"Why wouldn't you tell me about it? Or even try to stop it?"

"Oh, come on, it's just the stupid school paper," he says. "You can't possibly care about this."

"I don't care about this," I respond, driving my finger into the paper. "I care about you trying to make me look stupid."

"Well," he says, raising his eyebrows, "I'm not the one defunding every club who submits their annual budget requests."

"Yeah, well, sorry, man. I'm not going to keep giving these useless clubs handouts."

"I don't know what you want me to say," he says, rubbing his eyes.

"What I want you to say is 'thank you.'"

"I'm sorry?"

"You said it yourself in our last budget meeting, we've never had a bigger surplus!" I yell, louder than I mean to. My face feels hot.

"Yeah, but not because you're doing anything creative." He pauses and leans back in his chair before adding, "Anyone could do what you're doing."

I feel the adrenaline shooting through my body and before I can stop myself, I stand up and swipe my hand across his desk, sending all his papers, pens, and stupid tchotchkes hurtling to the ground. "I quit!" I roar, my voice echoing in the room as silence falls once more.

James stares at me, his mouth wide. I turn, walk quickly to my desk, gather my things, and run out the door, my fists clenched and jaw tight. I feel like I could run around the world, powered by rage alone. I can't wait to get into a fighter jet so I can climb as far above this place as possible, finally gliding into the position I deserve.

Three hours, fifteen loops around campus, and a few pipes later, I am sitting on a table in the school physician's office in a medical gown. After I ran out of the office, I scurried around trying to grab every school paper I could get my hands on. I wanted to burn them all but ended up throwing them into the dumpster behind the convenience store on campus instead. I can't expect simpletons to understand how politics work, nor can I stop them from being so sensitive about things that aren't personal. It's business, it's money, and by the way, I was doing an incredible job. Those ungrateful idiots will probably ride my success long after I graduate. I wonder if Donna has read the article yet. If she dumps me over this, I swear I'll find James on campus tomorrow and punch him in the face.

The doctor walks into the room, his shoes squeaking on the floor as he moves. "Robert Krulish?" he asks.

"Yes, you can call me Bob," I respond, reaching my hand out to shake his.

"Good to see you, sir." He reaches out and grabs my hand, offering a firm shake. "So, a physical for the fighter pilot training program? Exciting stuff," he says, his voice monotone.

"Yeah," I respond, upbeat. "It probably says there that the physical is a formality. I'm already in the program."

The doctor sits down to look at my file, and as he does, I hear the clicking of heels getting louder as someone approaches the room. Just then, the door flings open and a male voice shouts, "Krulish!"

It's Captain Baker. I straighten my back and move my hand to salute him, though I feel awkward doing so in a state of undress, "Sir!" I say.

"You've got some major explaining to do," he says. I notice he's holding a stack of papers and my stomach flips. He's heard about the article.

"Sir, I saw the article too. I was just as shocked as you are."

"Article? What are you talking about?" he says, then looks at the doctor, who offers a shrug.

"Maybe I'm confused," I respond.

"I think we're all confused, Krulish. What I have here are your transcripts. You're failing? You told me you had straight As."

I swallow hard.

"From what I see here," he begins, leafing through the papers for dramatic effect, "you haven't gotten an A in a very long time. You have more incompletes here than I've ever seen on a transcript."

"There must be some mistake," I say, though I know in the back of my mind he's right. "Let me go to the dean's office and talk to them."

"Listen, son," the captain says, placing the papers under his arm. "I'm hoping there's something wrong, that there's a big misunderstanding, and that these transcripts happen to belong to someone else, but my gut says there's no mistake. And if I'm right, which I usually am, son, you're not making it into this program. In fact, you might just be on your way out of UCF altogether."

My throat is tight, but I muster a "Yes, sir." Then I add, "I'll make sure you get the correct transcripts as soon as possible."

"I need them yesterday," he says.

"Yes, sir," I say, with a final salute. He locks eyes with me for another moment before turning on his heels and leaving the room.

"Okay," the doctor says, breaking the silence. "Let's get on with it."

It, I think, in, insect, instinct, insight, inflict, innocent, imposter.

I walk into my dorm room to find my roommate, Benjamin, lying on his bed listening to Led Zeppelin. It's his favorite band and he's had Led Zeppelin II on repeat all semester. The music is so loud it's piercing every thought that comes into my head. I am rifling through my closet looking for my nice shirt and tie. My hands land on a golf shirt, which I pull out and hold up on the hanger. It's wrinkled, but I think it'll do for dinner. I pull off my T-shirt and pull the golf shirt over my head. The music mingles with my twisted thoughts, causing rage to churn beneath the surface. Words bubble inside me until they burst, like magma from a volcano. "Turn this down!" I bellow. Benjamin doesn't react.

I grab my toiletry case and stomp to the bathroom, where I place myself in front of the mirror. I reach for the sink handle and turn it too hard, sending water spraying out of the faucet. I look down. My shirt is wet. I ball my left hand into a fist and slam it down on the sink. Pain shoots through my hand and I close my eyes tight, wishing the building would explode. I open my eyes, grab my comb, wet it, and run it through my hair. As I do, I make eye contact with myself in the mirror and, for the first time, notice something undeniable. Though my hair is brown, it is slicked back like my dad's always was after a shower or in the morning when he appeared after a night away. My jaw is clenched, my lips tight, eyes wild. I look like him.

I replay the sound of the items from James's desk crashing onto the floor, the sting of my hands as they hit the metal desk, the roar of my voice. I retrace my steps as I lied to Captain Baker and the lump in my throat that formed right away. I recall the feeling of yelling at Benjamin, the pain of punching the sink. I shake these impressions as my brain is flooded with thoughts about my reality. I am nothing like my dad. I have a beautiful girlfriend who loves me. I am a senator on the student government, and no idiot loser is going to change the good I've done. I belong in the fighter pilot program. I deserve a spot and I will get it. Forget my transcripts; those things are meaningless anyway. I'm so far beyond books, attendance sheets, and grades. They'll come to their senses and I'll be in an F-14A running drills in a matter of days. I splash water on my face and feel instantly better. I am filled with energy and excitement so powerful, I feel like I've had a shot of espresso or four. I want to high-five the world.

I leave the bathroom and head back to my room. Benjamin is still on his bed and the music still blares. "Hey, man," I say. "Sorry about before."

"It's fine. I'm used to your crap," he says with a smirk.

"What's with the volume? Something happen?" I ask.

"Stacey broke up with me," he says, rubbing his eyes.

"Man, that sucks," I say, patting him on the shoulder.

"Yeah. I don't know what her damage is."

"Well, I do. It seems like she doesn't know who you are. You're Benjamin! You're a catch! You don't need her. You'll find another, better girl. You know what you need? You need to rock it out!" I gesture toward the record player and he cranks the volume even higher. Together, we play air guitar and jump around the room. With each jump, I feel like I might crash through the ceiling and shoot into the universe. This day doesn't matter anyway. What even is a day? Once you've experienced it, it's practically history, and history should stay in the past where it belongs.

I reach out and offer Benjamin a high five. He slaps my hand with satisfying force. I head out of the room with a wave and bound down the stairs, out the door, and break into a run. I'm moving faster than I ever have, headed toward Donna's dorm at record speed. My heart is racing, my chest is heaving, my legs are burning. I picture myself like a blur of color, racing past people like a fighter jet on the runway.

I arrive at the door of Donna's dorm in less than ten minutes. It usually takes me fifteen. I see her through the glass door as she makes her way toward me. Her hair is perfectly straight, like strands of luminous string made of pure gold; her dress is pressed; her black shoes bright and shiny. She has a small leather bag over her shoulder and a denim jacket over one arm. As she comes toward me, I smell her perfume in the breeze and break into a smile so big it feels like my cheeks are about to crack. She stops just in front of me, stands on tiptoes, and kisses me before taking my hand. She looks me in the eye, her brow furrowed. "You doing okay?" she asks.

"I'm great!" I say. "Hungry, but great!"

"Good," she says, her mouth curling into a familiar, easy smile. "I was worried after I saw the paper. Those idiots don't know what they're talking about."

"Oh, I know!" I said, waving my hand. "I really haven't thought much about it."

"I'm so glad. My dad deals with bad press like that a lot. You just have to let it roll off your back."

"Yep, like I said, I barely gave it a second thought."

"Well, I'm proud of you. And the physical?"

"Exactly like I thought. Just a formality!"

"That's wonderful. I'm happy for you!"

I grab her hand and tug, pulling her toward the parking lot, and say, "Let's go. We shouldn't be late."

"Wow, you're energetic tonight," she says, jogging slightly to keep up with me. "Have a lot of caffeine today?" She laughs.

"I'm good!" I say. "I just love you, that's all."

"Can we slow down a bit?" she calls out. "I'm in heels!"

I notice that I'm holding her hand and jogging in front of her like an eager leashed puppy on the way to the park. I slow my pace but continue to jog by her side.

When we get to my car, I open the door for her. She gets in and I close the door enthusiastically. I think about the fact that I drive a car my dad left behind at his mom's house and I imagine him driving it when he took girls on dates. I run to the driver's side, yank the door open, and sit down in the driver's seat. I rev the engine and without pausing to look behind me, I step down hard on the gas, sending us hurtling out of the parking spot, then put the car in drive and step on the gas again. We fly forward, moving eighty miles per hour out of the lot. We race down the street and I press my foot on the gas pedal even harder, pushing it until I feel the floorboard making contact beneath it. We're racing past building after building, the neon lights blending together in bright, bold swirls.

"Why are you driving so fast?" Donna yells.

I look over and she's hanging on to the roof handle with one hand and is fumbling to fasten her seat belt with the other. It suddenly registers that she looks scared. I slam my foot on the brake. As silence falls over the car, she looks at me, her eyes wide with terror. My body tenses as I wait for her reaction. I think she's going to yell and scream, call me names, get out of the car and slam the door. Instead, she catches her breath, puts her hand on my knee and says, "Are you sure you're okay?"

My shoulders drop. I place my hand on hers and say, "I'm good, I'm sorry. Just having a little fun."

She inhales sharply. "I get it, but I'd like to live to eat dinner, okay?"

"Got it," I say, easing my foot onto the gas pedal.

She tucks her hair behind her ears, smoothens her dress, and says, "You weren't lying."

"What do you mean?" I respond.

"You're definitely qualified to fly a fighter jet." She looks at me, eyebrow raised, and adds, "No training necessary."

* * *

I carefully ease the car into the driveway of Donna's parents' house. Never is the rust on my dad's old Firebird more apparent to me than it is against the backdrop of her family's sweeping estate. I turn off the engine and Donna and I both step out of the car, close our doors, then join hands and walk toward the front door of the house. We stop at the threshold and she straightens her dress, turns to me, and adjusts my collar.

"There, she says," then reaches for the doorknob and turns it. The light inside is bright, yet comforting, and the smell of steak, sherry, and onions wafts through the air. There is the tinkling sound of a piano playing in the background. Donna places her purse and jacket on a bench by the door and calls out, "Hi, Mom! Hi, Dad! We're here!"

"Hey, Sprout!" her dad booms as he walks into the foyer in an expertly pressed suit, tailored to perfection. He hugs Donna, then extends his hand to shake mine and says, "Bob! Great to see you."

I shake his hand firmly and say, "Great to see you too!"

"Staying busy?" he asks.

"Busier than ever, sir. Budget season at school, lots to review."

"Oh, man," he says with a chuckle. "I know how that is. I hope you're running a tight ship."

"I am, sir." I give him a knowing smile and continue, "People really don't like it when you make them work for their money."

"You'll love this, Dad," Donna interrupts. My throat tightens as she says, "Bob got his first piece of bad press today. The school paper printed a nasty article about him cutting funding."

"Bad press, you say?" I brace myself for his response. "Well, Bob. Sounds like you really are ready for the big leagues. Come on, son. Let me pour you a drink."

As we walk to the bar, Donna's mom comes down the stairs. Her blond hair is teased and sprayed in place. She is wearing a hot pink skirt suit—the jacket's shoulder pads are so crisp, they almost look sharp. "Hello, you sweet young couple," she says with a smile. She walks over to Donna, wraps her arms around her, and says, "You look beautiful, honey! Oh my. Looks like Daddy has the scotch out before dinner. Are we celebrating?" She glances down at Donna's left hand.

"Not exactly," I say.

"Oh, yes, we are," handing her a glass, "Our Bob had a scathing article written about him in the school paper today. Budget cuts!"

"Well, cheers to that," she says, raising a glass.

"To Bob!" Donna says. "Who not only received his first piece of bad press today but also took the final step on his path to the UCF fighter pilot training program!"

"Wow!" Her dad whoops as we bring our glasses together. "That's fantastic news! I can't imagine things going better for you right now."

Euphoric excitement rushes through my veins as I notice the adoration on their faces. Before I can stop myself I add, "That's right. And I'll be on the dean's list this semester too."

"Well, then. Seems like you really deserve this delicious dinner we're about to have!" Donna's mom says, placing her hand on my back to signal that we should make our way to the table.

Together we walk toward the dining room, laughing and talking about the future and what it'll be like to live in a house like theirs one day. When I speak to them, I gloss over the poverty I knew my whole life. Instead, I tell them their house reminds me of the home I grew up in. I paint the picture of a happy childhood, parents in love, hardworking father, doting mother, scrappy siblings.

As we sit down at the table, a familiar family portrait on the wall catches my eye. I stop and squint at it, imagining myself in it, just behind Donna, to the right of her older brother. I am there in a navy-blue suit and red tie, my hand on Donna's shoulder. I blink hard and I'm still there in the photo, smiling back at myself, looking positively presidential. With every inch of my being, I know that's my future. I know I'm destined for greatness beyond anything my family has ever known. And I know exactly what I need to do to make it happen.

Chapter 9

THIS DOESN'T LOOK GREAT

'm sitting on a bench outside the dean's office just as the sun begins to peek over the horizon. Birds are slowly coming to life one by one, calling to one another to signal the start of a new day. I didn't sleep last night. Not for one minute. My mind was too busy running different scenarios. I got sick of tossing and turning at around 2 a.m., got out of bed, and came here to dig through my thoughts and wait for the office to open. I had to think through every possible outcome of going to the dean's office, every argument they could make and every way I could counter those arguments effectively. Technically, no, I haven't been going to class, but that doesn't mean I'm not the best student at this school. If nothing else, I'll get them to write a letter about me being on the dean's list. That should be enough to please Captain Baker. Then, I'll just walk into the student government building like nothing happened. Everyone knows politicians have a short fuse. Who cares that I lost it on James? Not me.

Slowly, the campus starts to reawaken. First, joggers run past, their ponytails bouncing with each step. Then, students start to emerge, eyes sleepy, hands laced around thermoses filled with hot coffee. The sun is bright now, the morning rays of light gleaming on the plush green grass illuminating the glistening dewdrops. A young woman approaches the building. Her skin is dark and her tightly curled hair bounces with each step. She is neatly dressed in a crisp, white-collared shirt and is clutching a briefcase in one hand and a coffee in the other. She stops at the door, cradles her coffee in her left elbow, which seems risky, and digs in her bag with her right hand. This is my chance. I stand, jog over to her, and call out, "Excuse me! Can I help you with that?"

She jumps and locks eyes on me then replies, "Sure, thanks," while handing me her coffee.

"No problem," I respond. "Hey, do you happen to work in the dean's office?"

"I do," she replies.

"Awesome. I'm Bob and I need some help. Can I follow you in?"

She pulls her keys from the bottom of her bag and unlocks the door before taking her coffee cup from my hand and responding, "Sure, but I have to warn you, I've only had two sips of this coffee. I can't be blamed for anything I say that you don't like."

"Understood," I say with a chuckle.

I follow her in and tell her the story about Captain Baker showing up at my physical. I explain that, sure, I've missed classes, but I was a part of the student government and was really working hard. I tell her about the budget cuts, about the school paper and how silly the article was, and about the fact that I'd be a US senator one day soon. She listens patiently as she steps behind the counter, places her bag by her chair, and goes straight for the filing cabinet. She runs her fingers over the files in the drawer, then pulls one out that I assume is mine. Her skirt swishes as she walks back to the counter. She opens the folder and drums her nails as she flips through the pages. She takes a deep breath in before she says, "Bob, I'll be honest. This doesn't look great."

"How so?" I ask.

"Frankly, I'm surprised you have to ask that question."

"What do you mean?"

"Well, it looks like you had a great first semester, had straight As, were on the dean's list and everything. But beyond that, it looks like things haven't gone so well."

"Are you kidding? Things have gone great. Just ask anyone in student government."

"Okay, but student government is extracurricular. When it comes to classes, you've accomplished next to nothing." She closes the folder, then continues, "I'm not even sure how you're still enrolled here. It looks like you haven't been to a single class all semester."

"What does that matter?"

"I'm confused as to what you think college is for exactly. This is an institution of learning. If you don't want to go to class, then why are you here?"

"My transcript shows exactly why I'm here—for the programs, the teams, the trainings."

"These programs are intended for elite students."

"I am an elite student. I'm on the dean's list!"

"No, you were an elite student during your first semester here. Ever since, well, I can't see evidence that you've done much at all." She picks up her coffee and takes a sip, staring at me the whole time.

I feel it bubble inside me again—the white-hot anger threatening to explode. I stand there with my teeth clenched, desperately fighting to stay calm. I could lose it on a colleague. I could lose it on a friend. But someone in the dean's office? No. Not here. I force myself to breathe. Finally, through clenched teeth I say, "Is there anything you can do to help me?"

"Unfortunately, no. There's nothing I can do. And I have to prepare you for the reality of what's coming next. You're likely going to be asked to leave the school."

Her words hit me like fists in my gut landing over, and over, and over. I want to grab the folder from the counter, throw it on the floor, and scream. But I stand still trying to figure out my next move. My brain is flooded with things I could do and say, thoughts are coming so fast it feels like a fleet of freight trains are speeding through my mind. I can't latch on to one single thought, so I mutter, "Thanks for nothing," and stomp out of the office.

I walk back outside feeling nothing and everything all at once. People are beginning to come to the office now. They step around me, rushing to get to their stupid meetings about stupid classes that mean nothing. And here I am in last night's clothes—the clothes I wore to celebrate my future—yet now, I have no future to speak of thanks to some rigged, corrupt educational system. For a moment, I think about trying to go back inside and try to see the dean himself, but what's the point? It seems like everyone is out to get me and if that's the case, he'll be in on it too. Then, for a moment, it makes sense. I am well on my way to becoming a US senator. The dean can't have someone like me around making him look weak and unaccomplished. Of course he wants me gone. Fine. I'll just leave, conquer the world on my own, and show them. College or no college, I am destined for great things. I am Bob Krulish, the kangaroo, ketchup, kaleidoscope, kayak, knee jerk, King of the Universe. They'll just have to wait and see.

Chapter 10

BREAKING CODE

I am sitting in my car in the parking lot of the Colonial Shopping Plaza on a sunny Friday afternoon. I watch as eager shoppers dart in and out of stores getting the food they need for weekend barbecues and boat trips. My heart beats quickly as I look through the crowd and eye my destination, which is buried just between the Casual Corner clothing store and a Michael's craft store. A once-empty storefront is now occupied by a group of US Army Reserve members who are looking to recruit new members. In the last week, I've walked past the office several times trying to get a sense of what it was all about. Each time, I saw uniformed men with tightly cropped haircuts milling around, sometimes talking to potential recruits, sometimes palling around in a way that seems unique to brothers in arms. On my last trip past the storefront, they'd put out a new poster. The slogan on it read, "Train Here, Succeed Anywhere." I already feel like I am capable of succeeding anywhere. With army training, I'd be unstoppable. Not only that, but I overheard one of the officers telling someone that they were offering $2,000 to all new recruits. Apparently, with Vietnam barely in the rearview, they basically had to bribe people to sign up. Fine with me. I can only imagine what it'll feel like to have so much money in hand. I know exactly what I'll do with it too. I've heard of guys taking $2,000 and turning it into millions by investing wisely. That's something I can do with my eyes closed. I just know it.

I haven't spoken to Donna in a month. Not since I officially found out I was being kicked out of school. Not since I lost student government, had to walk away from the training program, and had to move off campus. I hope she thinks I ran off with another girl. I hope she believes that I became so successful that I had to bail on college. Maybe she thinks I got an amazing job somewhere or that I was just busy flying planes in the program.

For a while, I tried to fake it for Donna. I tried to pretend that everything was okay and that things were moving forward as planned. Even though I left the dorms almost right away, I tried to make her think I was still living there by switching up our routine. I offered to meet her at her dorm more often, pretended that my "meeting schedules" were different, and that training was taking up a ton of time, but soon it all became too much. I couldn't break up with her because I didn't want to tell her the truth, or even a shadow of the truth, so I just stopped seeing her altogether. Even now, I try to pretend like I don't care, but in the dead of night, as I try to sleep in my back seat, I am kept awake by memories of her smell. But I can't face what I've done. Not with Donna or with anyone else, including my mom. I can't bear to think about the weight of the disappointment she's carrying because of me.

I look around my car and try to figure out a way to make myself look presentable. I fish around in the front seat for the leather bag Donna's parents had given me as a gift last Christmas. I dump out its contents and begin packing items into it that I can use to freshen up. Deodorant, a toothbrush and toothpaste, my comb, a collared shirt from the floor of the back seat, and a few folders and books, which I'll leave in the bag as props. I step out of the car, lock the door, and head into the grocery store. I walk straight to the bathroom where I put on the shirt and tuck it into my pants before heading to the sink where I freshen up. I had forgotten a razor, so I decide that I need to work with the long stubble that's been growing since I left school. I lock eyes with myself while combing my hair. It's the right thing to do, joining the reserves, and once I do, I might finally be able to face my mom again.

I leave the bathroom, exit the store, and head for the storefront where the reserves are set up. I open the heavy metal door and step through it into the crisp air-conditioned room, walk straight to the front table, and begin filling out a form. My pen flies as I list my experience as a leader who did unprecedented work for my school's student government, a trainee in the fighter pilot training program, and a straight-A student.

The mop glides across the floor like an eager skater over a patch of fresh ice. The air in the barracks is thick and hot, coating my skin with a slick layer of moisture. My shirt and pants are always stuck to my skin, making me feel like a mummy rotting beneath layers of cloth bandages. I want to peel off my clothes and run through soft white sand into bubbly surf, dive beneath the waves, and swim until I reach the horizon.

I dunk the mop into the murky water and notice that I feel angry. Not just now—every single time I head to the janitor's closet and roll the bucket out of its resting place. Quite frankly, these chores are beneath me. They're so far beneath me that I shouldn't even be in the same room as someone mopping. Once I was accepted into the reserves, I had to take the ASVAB, or Armed Services Vocational Aptitude Battery, a test used to determine qualifications and proper placement. Once the recruiter scored my test, he looked at me in disbelief and said, "Nobody's ever scored this high on the ASVAB that I've ever recruited in my life." I didn't tell him that it was because he'd never recruited anyone like me, The Answer Key. It turns out I qualified for one of the most elite jobs that exists in the Army Reserves—working with the air force in cryptography. After my advanced training, I would sit in the back of a plane and would be flown over war zones to intercept messages and decode them. I would be like the hero in every great action movie ever made. Eat that, Captain Baker.

The only caveat was that I had to make it through basic training first and it's nothing like I thought it would be. Because I had an associate's degree, I was made private first class—a squad leader. Thanks to army posters, movies, and action figures, I believed the army was comprised of elite soldiers hand-selected from the upper echelon of American society. I imagined being alongside big, buff, brainy guys like myself, training hard to become skilled fighting machines, training guys beneath me who were clean-cut and respectable. Instead, I'm leading a squad of knuckleheads alongside other squad leaders who were a bunch of deadbeats, bums, and ex-cons. At first, I had to push aside lingering fears that they'd request my transcripts from UCF, find out about my incompletes, and can me. It turns out one semester on the dean's list in college makes me the most scholastically accomplished guy here by a million miles.

Now, everyone is doing their morning chores, rushing to get the room clean, their beds made, and their shoes shined before 5 a.m. I look down and notice that I'm barely halfway through the job and know for a fact that I won't finish before it's time to get out on the green and run before morning chow. Running presented its own problems. Weeks of crawling through mud, dragging a fifty-pound rucksack, and doing sprints have aggravated an old injury. Now, my knee is puffy and painful, making it tough to function normally. I dunk the mop into the bucket one last time and swish it across the floor twice more before pushing the bucket back into the closet. I look back at the floor. It's blatantly obvious that I haven't finished my work but I don't care. There's only so much I can get done and I didn't join the reserves to do stupid chores like this.

I look at my watch. It's 4:59, time to get outside for our run. I inhale sharply through my nose as the clock flips to 5:00. Right on schedule, the sergeant pushes the door open and yells, "Line up!"

There is a flurry of fast, coordinated activity and all forty men form two lines. We march out of the barracks and onto the yard where the air is just as thick and heavy. The sergeant shouts commands and we pick up the pace accordingly. I watch as heads bob in front of me, all uniformly shaped, hair meticulously cropped around each set of ears. I try to ignore the shooting pain in my knee, but with each step, it gets a little worse. I try to channel the pain, to think about something that makes me angry, to check out of the situation and go somewhere else. I think about my dad. I think about where he could be and what he could be doing. I imagine him sipping cocktails with Maureen. I imagine his skin leathery and tan, his face relaxed and happy. Then I remember every time he called me an idiot, told me I was stupid, made me feel worthless. I think about Kryse's eyes, angrily staring through me, as if I had made my dad act like a jerk toward Rik. I think about my mom's face and how it fell into a deep, mournful frown every time my dad chose not to come home. I think about that frown and how it set up permanent residence on her face once he left for good. I think about how I waited to talk to her after leaving school until I had something redeeming to tell her. I remember her face curling into a grimace and the sobs she let out when I told her I joined the reserves. She worried intensely that I'd be taken from her—that, somehow, lingering effects of Vietnam would cause me to get drafted—something I hadn't even considered. I feel a rush of anger. With it comes a rush of energy and I pick up my pace for a moment, placing myself on the heels of the person in front of me. I try to right my pace and stumble on my own foot. It's a tiny misstep but it's enough to send pain shooting from my knee up my thighs and into the trunk of my body. I shriek and fall to the ground waving to the sergeant. The rest of the group keeps running.

"Sir, I can't run anymore. It's my knee," I say, breathless.

He looks back at me with his eyes squinted. He breathes in like he's about scream at me. I brace myself, then he yells, "Everybody stop!"

"Sergeant, you don't need to…" I start.

He interrupts me and says, "Oh no, I insist." Then, he turns to the group and continues, "Krulish can't run anymore. So we're all going to take a break and we're going to let Krulish rest his leg. While he takes a break, the rest of you will do fifty push-ups. Actually, no. I noticed he didn't get the floors done this morning either. Must also be that bad knee of his. How about you all give Krulish one hundred to make that knee feel better. Krulish, you stand up and don't do anything. The men will do them for you."

The men drop to the ground and start doing push-ups. I watch as their heads bob up and down, knowing that they're all wishing I'd drop dead with each push-up they do. I try to keep my face steady, but the pain combined with the knowledge that I'll probably get my behind kicked when nobody is looking makes me feel like I can't breathe. Then, I remember, that's the drill sergeant's goal. To make me feel like I'm out of control—to scare me into submission. Well, he doesn't know who he's dealing with. If I haven't been broken before, I won't be broken now. I'm an intellectual commodity. I'm an elite human being. And, maybe, this is how it should be. Maybe these soldiers should be doing push-ups on my behalf. After all, one day, I'll be decoding messages that will save their lives and the lives of their sad, sorry families. They should be thanking me with way more than a few pathetic push-ups.

<hr />

I am sitting at a desk with nothing but a notebook and a pen. There is a soldier in front of me at a similar desk with a radio and a blank sheet of paper. He is wearing headphones. He scribbles furiously, then hands a paper back to me that reads, "Two tennis balls with Jason, a cheese sub down a freeway. There was a clown, a mountain center, and a cockroach in the car." Then there is a small note in the corner that says, "Russian accent."

I tap my foot as I read the words again and again, looking for any way into the code. I think about exactly what I am hearing. I've decoded things from Russian transmissions before. My brain races to recall the messages I have figured out. There was one about a submarine, one about an attack on one of their borders, and one about a tank. That's it! I think. Cheese sub is a rough translation. The word should be pizza, which is the word they've been using for tank. It's a tank. My pencil flies. I raise my hand and the sergeant comes to my desk. He reads the paper, looks at the clock, and says, "You'll be in the air in no time."

—⁂—

I am sitting in the mess hall at an empty table with my tray in front of me. My stomach churns with hunger, though I grimace at the food. The thought of eating a mouthful of lumpy, powdered mashed potatoes makes me feel sick. I force myself to take a bite and wash it down with room-temperature juice. I imagine what it would be like to be in prison and wonder if it would actually be better than the reserves. I look over at a table that has filled up with a group of squad leaders. One of them glances over at me and whispers something to the guy sitting beside him. They both look at me and burst into laughter. I can't believe these are the people I'm stuck with. They're total buffoons. After a day of pouring over transmissions, putting my brain through rigorous training, it seems wrong to be here surrounded by the lowest of the low with a knee the size of a soccer ball. The smaller of the two looks back at me and makes eye contact. He stares at me, expressionless, then leans in and says something to the group. They all nod.

Great, I think.

Several hours later after training wraps up for the day, I lie awake in my bunk. My knee is aching and I jump at every small sound. At some point, I think about golf. I imagine myself free of injury, walking the biggest course I've ever seen. The grass is emerald green, the breeze is light and cool. I stop and place my ball on the tee, and just as I lift my club, I am startled awake by a serpentine whisper: "Yo, college."

"What the…" I say, sitting up quickly. As my eyes focus, I realize that I must have dropped off for a moment and now I'm surrounded by the other squad leaders, who must have been waiting to pounce.

One of them sits down on the edge of my bunk and grabs me by the shirt, gets close to my face, and hisses, "Looks like that fancy college learning of yours didn't cover everything."

"Guys," I say, trying to sound relaxed, "I don't know what you want me to say. My knee is messed up."

"Everyone's got something messed up," one of them hisses.

"Yeah," the one on my bed spits, "I have a bad shoulder, Wilson there has a messed-up back, we've all got something."

"Just look," I say, reaching down. I pull up my pant leg, which will barely budge over my knee. When I finally get it up far enough, there is a collective gasp.

"Dang," one of them says as he leans into my bunk. His breath smells like cigarettes and beef jerky.

"I told you," I say, pulling my pant leg down again.

"You have to talk to the sergeant and get that drained. You can't just act like you can keep up. You'll keep bailing and we'll keep taking the blows for you."

"I get it, and I'll talk to him."

I look at their faces and notice that the anger they'd approached me with has melted into something that looks like sympathy.

Chapter 11

CHASING DREAMS

Water from the faucet cascades over the dish, soaking my pruning hands as I scrub. I stare out the window into the backyard. It is twilight and fireflies are beginning to dance, scattered across the yard like a miniature galaxy of twinkling stars. I place the dish in the rack, then reach for a pan, flip the sponge over, and use the abrasive side to scrub the last of the cheese off the bottom.

Training wrapped several weeks ago and I'm still getting used to being back home. With training under my belt, I know I could be called to serve at any time, but I doubt that will happen anytime soon. With the nation weary from war, no one is looking to fight any longer. With no war zones to fly over, there are far fewer messages to decode, which means all the work can be done by seasoned professionals. I am therefore left to reenter society, my new qualifications and my newly drained knee making me feel like a better version of myself. Though my mom still harbors fear that there will be some resurgence of war and I'll be called away, she now seems proud of my training, often commenting on how happy she is to have me back by her side.

She now sits at the kitchen table just a few feet away. Her elbow is resting next to a jumble of unpaid bills. She holds one in her hand and studies it as if she's looking for some small error that will vindicate her from the debt she finds herself in. She sighs, puts the paper down, and says, "I think I'm going to make a cup of tea. Want one?"

"Sure," I say, placing the pan in the drying rack.

She grabs the kettle from the stove, walks to the sink, and fills it. The water makes a tinny splashing sound as it hits the bottom of the kettle. She places her hand on my back, looks at me, and says, "Thank you for cleaning up from dinner."

"Of course," I say, wiping the remaining water out of the sink and off the counter. I fold the dish towel and place it on the edge of the sink and sit down at the table.

"Listen," my mom says, turning on the stove and placing the kettle on the burner, "I'm just barely making ends meet here. I know you plan to contribute, but I think there might be better options for us elsewhere."

My stomach flips. "Let me guess. You want to be closer to Rik and Kryse?"

"Not just them. I have friends in California. Family too." She rifles through the cabinet until her hand lands on a box of tea bags.

"This isn't just some excuse to get out there, is it? I know why Rik went in the first place. It's ridiculous."

My mom places a tea bag in a mug for each of us, then turns to face me, leaning her back on the counter, crossing her arms in front of her chest. For the first time, I notice that she's starting to look old.

"I agree with you," she says. "It's a ridiculous situation. You and I went out every night for years looking for your dad and never found anything."

"Right, and Rik laughed at us every time we went out. Then, what? He just decides to pack up and move to California because he has it in his head that that's where Dad ended up? What would he even do if he found him?"

The kettle screams and my mom lifts it off the burner, then pours steaming water over the tea bags. She carefully picks up the mugs and walks to the table, placing one in front of me and one in front of herself as she sits down. She pushes the pile of bills out of the way, then says, "Look, I know it's crazy and I don't understand it either, nor do I get why Kryse ended up going out there too, but truthfully, it doesn't matter. Me saying we should go to California has nothing to do with them or with your father. It's a good place to live. The money is better and I have connections that can help us get great jobs. It'd be a fresh start. I think we could both use one of those."

"I know." My face feels hot. "I hope you don't secretly think I'm a failure."

"A failure?" She reaches across the table and puts her warm hand on mine.

"Yeah," I say, shifting in my chair.

"Oh, Bobby. Listen, do I like that you joined the reserves with the war barely wrapped up? Absolutely not. Does it make me happy that you were kicked out of school? No. But I'd never, ever consider you a failure, son."

"Thanks," I say, taking my hand out from under hers. "So, let's say we do go to California. What's the plan?"

"Well, Aunt Mae has been asking me to come out to San Jose. She cleans houses out there. She makes so much money, you really wouldn't believe it."

"So, you're going to clean houses?" I ask.

"Oh, goodness no," she says, sipping her tea. She places the mug back on the table. "It's way better than that. You know Smith Brothers?"

"The stockbrokers?"

"Yes! Mae works for someone who is really high up at the company. She thinks they'll hire me as a secretary."

"Really? Wow, that could be great." I blow on my tea, then add, "But what would I do?"

"Let's not worry too much about that. You never have a problem finding work." She wrinkles her brow and continues, "You know, no matter what I do, this house will always be a place where something terrible happened to me—to us. This is the place where we came when your father abandoned us. It's the place where all my dreams of being a perfect, white-picket-fence, golden-retriever family died. Sometimes it feels like living in a dumpster that's just overflowing with my broken dreams. I think it's time to move on."

I knew what she meant. Although it had been ten years since my dad practically threw us out of his moving car, the place still feels sad. It is still filled with the same old hand-me-down furniture. The same rotary phone my mom would fall asleep next to, waiting for my dad to call, still sits on a side table in the living room. The carpet is worn and stained from years of Rik and Kryse playing rough, tracking mud inside, and spilling food while they ate diners in front of the TV.

"Okay," I say. "Let's do it!"

"You mean it?" she says, clapping excitedly.

"I mean it. Let's go."

She jumps up and hugs me, bumping the table with her hip, causing tea to splash out of the cup and onto the splintering wood.

━━━

In the grand tradition of my family, we are in the car on our way to San Jose barely a week later. Only this time, there is no uncertainty hanging in the air. This trip is filled with happiness so pure and exhilarating, I can't help but drum the dashboard, sing along to our old eight-track tapes, and let my hand ride the wind that whooshes around our car. My mom does the same, her hair flying, eyes smiling behind her old gas-station aviator sunglasses. We snack on Sour Patch Kids, Cow Tails, and Big League Chew. Once in a while, we mime smoking with candy cigarettes and sip Big Gulps, which we find can take a full day to finish.

My mom and I fall into a steady rhythm as the days go by. We know the trip will take five days and we're okay with taking it slower, or faster, depending on how things go on any given day.

We wake up in our motel room before the sun comes up and pile into the car, chipper despite the early hour. We switch driving throughout the day, but I go first, piloting us as my mom sips motel coffee and leafs through whatever local paper she bought for a quarter in the lobby at checkout.

This morning, on day three of our drive, I watch as the sun rises slowly, first peeking gingerly over the horizon then seemingly bursting the rest of the way all at once. I think about everything we're headed toward. I think about wealth. I think about myself in the same yard I used to picture myself in with Donna. Only now, I picture myself standing alone after a long day, a scotch in one hand and a hose in the other. I am watering my lawn, caring for my kingdom. I am king of the castle. I am ruler of the roost. I am happy.

Chapter 12

DIALING FOR DOLLARS

A crisp pacific breeze swirls around me as I walk through the parking lot and into the Smith Brothers Stockbrokers' building in downtown San Jose. I have come here to pick my mom up from work every day since she started her job more than a month ago. Today, however, I am here for a different, better reason—an interview that I am ready to knock out of the park.

Working in the wire department, my mom comes into contact with dozens of people in the office each day. Everyone was friendly to her right away because they knew she was hired by Dan, the vice president of the company who employed Aunt Mae as his housekeeper. Last Tuesday, she ran into Dan in the hallway and spoke to him about me. She explained my background and he said he had an opening on his team and wanted to meet me. "No promises," he told her, a phrase that I always took as a personal challenge.

I have never been more prepared for or more pumped about an interview in my life. I know for a fact that I'm about to get this job and that it's going to lead to wealth beyond my wildest dreams. As the reception-ist walks me back, I imagine myself in a cherry-red Porsche convertible with my beautiful, blond wife in the front seat. She laughs, looks at me, then puts her hands in the air before I slam on the gas. We zoom into the sunset and I come back to the present just as the receptionist ushers me into Dan's office.

He greets me with a firm handshake, takes my resume from me, and sits, motioning for me to take a seat as well. My eyes drift around his office as he stares intently at my resume. My eyes land on a photo on his desk of him, his wife, and their children, posing together on a beach. They stare back at me, relaxed, sun-kissed smiles on their faces.

Dan breaks the silence. "Well, Bob. How about we get right to it?"

"Sure!" I say, upbeat.

"I like your mom. And it seems like you've got some good experi-ence—military, too. I like that. But why should I hire you if you've got no experience with finance at all?"

"I get it," I say, laughing. "But how about I counter that with a ques-tion for you?"

He raises an eyebrow, smiles, and says, "Okay, why not?"

"Is it better to train someone to do a job exactly the way you want it done, or is it better to hire someone with a bunch of terrible habits you have to get them to break?"

He chuckles, then says, "Touché. But I can't teach you everything you need to know for a job like this. Most of the guys on my team have master's degrees."

"I'm sure they do. But what they don't have is my mind. Did you know, at UCF, I was elected to student government as a treasurer and I became senator within a few weeks. That's never been done before. Then I wanted to get into the fighter pilot program and I did that, no problem. But instead of going through the training, I joined the reserves to serve my country." I lean forward, then continue, "Dan, I scored higher on the

ASVAB than anyone the recruiter I worked with has ever scored. I bet you anything that if you let me take the Series 7 exam, I'll pass it."

Dan laughs and says, "I like your confidence."

"Thank you," I say. "And I'll prove to you that the reason I'm confident is that I don't fail."

"The Series 7 is no joke."

"With all due respect, neither am I, sir."

"Okay, then. Here's what we're going to do. There's a stockbroker training program that we offer and you have to pass the Series 7 to move ahead in the program. We set you up with study materials and even pay you for three months while you study. Then, you take the test and if you pass it with a 72 percent or better, you're in. You move into the office and get to start working on building your list of clients. Please don't get your hopes up though, Bob. We've never, ever let anyone without a bachelor's degree into the program. I can't imagine that we'll start now."

"I promise you, sir. I won't let you down."

I burst through the doors and forgo the elevator, choosing instead to run down all fifteen flights of stairs, slapping the railings with my hands. I feel electric, burning like a neon sign in the window of a twenty-four-hour diner. The happiness swirls in my chest, pushing against my face, pushing my mouth into a smile so big it feels like it will touch my eyes. It's finally happening. Someone has seen my talent, has admitted that my greatness is absolutely out of this world, and is giving me the chance I've always dreamed I'd get. I will eviscerate this test. I will get this job. I will become rich beyond my wildest dreams. And, one day, I will stare up at some poor sap from a photo on my desk. I'll be alone, happy, posing on the rolling hills of a pristine golf course, offering a steady reminder of what the good life really looks like.

Three months of pouring over books, cramming facts, and memorizing protocol flew by. And, of course, I passed the exam. How could anyone think I wouldn't? I showed up on test day ready to rock. Facts committed to memory, rules and regulations mastered. I showed up at the testing site and surveyed the guys competing with me. None of them looked like they stood a chance. I chose a desk at the front, sat down, and got to work as soon as they announced it was time to begin. None of the questions even came close to stumping me. There were a few that were more challenging than others, but in the end, I pulled it off. Dan was so impressed he could hardly believe that someone without a degree could pass.

Now, I'm approaching the building at warp speed. My feet are flying, bright, shiny shoes clicking against the pavement as I approach the revolving door. I am dressed to kill, my blue suit pressed with military precision, my pink shirt ironed, tie expertly knotted. My briefcase swings at my side—a glorified prop at this point since I only have my lunch to tote with me on my first day. I zoom through the revolving door and forgo the elevator in favor of the stairs. I jog up each flight, reciting facts I remember from the exam. I want to speak the language flawlessly.

I burst through the door at the fourteenth floor, walk quickly into the office, breeze past the receptionist, and walk up to Dan's open door and knock. He looks up and says, "There he is!"

"Dan, pleasure to see you," I say.

He shakes my hand, pats me on the shoulder, and says, "Let me show you to your seat." He walks me through a sea of desks in neat rows, each one occupied by someone speaking into a phone. I think back to my days in basic training, laughing to myself about the fact that none of the guys in my squad will ever get the chance to upgrade from jogging behind a row of bobbing heads to sitting in rows of desks like these.

We arrive at my desk. The surface is clear, except for a phone and a phone book. I place my briefcase on the floor and sit down in the rolling chair. "This is perfect, thanks."

"Great," Dan responds. "Nothing quite like being in the bullpen. Okay, I'll let you get settled, then we'll go over what you'll be doing day-to-day."

I look around the bullpen as Dan walks back to his office. I feel a sense of intense excitement wash over me. I'd spent so much of my life pretending to be rich that I often forgot how poor I really was. Now, I've finally made it. I am finally exactly where I belong, among exceptional, hardworking, high-earning people. Not only that, but I find myself among the top members of the staff, because I've clinched this spot without a college degree. I survey the room, counting each head I see, thinking about the years each employee must have spent pining to get here. The classes they sat through, the weeks of studying they did, the practice exams they took, and the sweat on their brows as they took the Series 7—the very same test I'd just breezed my way through. I clench my teeth, barely able to contain the sense of pure exhilaration that I feel.

I look to my right and catch the eye of the guy sitting next to me. He is in his twenties like me. His tie is loose around his neck and his head is tilted to the right as he talks into the receiver on his shoulder. "Great," he says, "I'm thrilled you'll be doing business with us. You'll receive an information packet in the mail this coming week. Wonderful. Speak with you soon." He hangs up the phone, turns to me, and says, "Nice shirt, I like the pink. First day?"

"Thanks. Yeah, I'm Bob," I say, then add, "Sounds like you made a sale. Congrats."

"All in a day's work, Bob. I'm Lyle," he says with a wave. "Training program?"

"Yes, just passed the test a few days ago."

"Nice," he said. "I'm in the program too. Me and six other guys around here. Well, seven other guys now. One sits behind you, Mark. Watch out for him." He picked up the receiver again, ran his finger down a page in the open phone book on his desk, and dialed.

My face falls a bit when I hear that so many others are in the program, but I shake the feeling. I know I'm in the top tier. How could I not be?

I turn around and see Mark sitting behind me. I catch his eye and offer him a wave. He looks nice enough. His hair is parted to one side, his white shirt tucked in, contrasting starkly with his black tie. I notice that he has a second book on his desk next to his open phone book. I squint to read the spine. The Bible. I stifle a laugh. A broker in training with a Bible on his desk might as well be carrying a sign that says "weakling."

———

After a quick meeting with Dan, I'm back at my desk staring at my copy of the phone book. In training the program, we start with zero clients. It's our responsibility through cold calling to get clients to open a CMA, or cash management account, which eventually gives us the cash to trade, which leads to a commission. I have a notebook on my desk and have written myself a script based on what Lyle says into the phone over and over throughout the day. Lyle is like a machine. He rarely puts the phone down. If he's at his desk, the phone is practically glued to his ear. He dials, speaks into the receiver, manually hangs up with his finger when he's done, then he dials again immediately. During his last cigarette break, I peeked at his desk and noticed he had a script scribbled on a sheet of paper in blue crayon. If he can do this, I can do it, no problem.

I pick up the receiver and open the phone book to a random page in the middle. I decide to start at the very top and work my way down the list. I dial the number and the phone rings, waiting for Mr. or Mrs. Mulder to answer. I hear crackling, then a female voice says, "Hello?"

"Hi there, is this Mrs. Mulder?"

"Yes," says the voice. "Who's this?"

"This is Bob calling with Smith Brothers. I'd like to talk to you about opening an account with us," I say, trying to mimic Lyle's voice exactly.

Click.

The line goes dead. I reach forward and dial the next number on the list. The phone rings and I wait for Mr. or Mrs. Mulderman to answer. A male voice answers this time. "Yes?"

"Hi there," I say, more upbeat this time. "Is this Mr. Mulderman?"

"This is he. Who's speaking?"

"This is Bob calling with Smith Brothers. I'd like to talk to you about opening an account with us," I say.

"Well, Bob with Smith Brothers," the voice at the other end booms, "I'd like to talk to you about the fact that you should get a real job. You're a real jerk, you know, interrupting my day like this."

"I…excuse me?" My stomach drops.

"No, sir. You excuse me. Where do you get off…"

Off, I think, on, open, opium, operation, option, opal.

I hang up the phone while Mr. Mulderman is still hurling insults at me. My heart is pounding. I look around the room and feel sudden shame. This kind of anger feels out of place in a setting like this. This can't be what people are hearing at the other end of the phone all day. I hear Lyle make sale after sale; I haven't heard him engaged in a single fight. He catches my eye, places his hand over the mouthpiece of his phone, which is glued to his ear as usual, and says, "Looks like you had a live one. It's okay, it's part of the job. Just hang up and move on to the next."

I give Lyle a thumbs-up as if that's what I'd planned to do all along. I stare at the phone and try to force myself to pick it up again but I can't. Instead, I pick up my pen and start flipping through the phone book pretending to strategically choose the next numbers I'll call. The anxiety is so strong I can hardly catch my breath. I stand up and walk to the bathroom. As the door closes behind me, I let the silence envelop me like a gentle hug. I glance at myself in the mirror and suddenly the blue suit and pink shirt I'd felt so good in look like a poorly constructed costume. Just then, the door swings open and a group of three established brokers walk in, all wearing designer suits and shiny shoes. One of them checks the stalls. They wave to me, then position themselves around one of the sinks in the middle of the restroom. One of them looks over at me and says, "Hey, new guy. You cool?"

"Of course," I respond instinctively.

"Good. You want some?"

I walk toward them and notice one of them holding a bag of white powder. The tallest one is sniffing through a hundred-dollar bill at a small pile on the edge of the sink. "Sure," I say.

"Nice. Think of it as a welcome gift. I'm Tom, this is Ryan and Cameron."

Tom opens the baggie and taps out a tiny pile of white powder onto the edge of the sink. Cameron hands me the rolled-up hundred-dollar bill. I lean over the sink, place the roll in my nose, and inhale. The powder burns as it hits the inside of my nostril but the discomfort is overshadowed by the jolt of euphoric energy that surges through my body. "Woo!" I exclaim.

The group shushes me and laughs collectively, then Ryan says, "I know, right—just keep it cool, buddy. We don't want any narcs finding out about this."

"Oh, don't worry," I say. "I'm cool. I wouldn't turn down a little bit more though."

Tom laughs, shrugs his shoulders and doles out one more small pile, then says, "I like your enthusiasm."

I put the rolled-up hundred-dollar bill back into my nose and sniff the fresh pile. This time, I don't even feel the burning, just the rush of beautiful, tingly rocket-fuel-like energy. I am dizzy with joy—as if I'd just sunk a hole in one, aced a test, and kissed a beautiful girl all in one millisecond. As the others finish taking their bumps off the backs of their hands, I pace around the bathroom. I can't believe I was worried about making those calls. I can handle a stupid phone call. I can make a million phone calls. I can make more calls than anybody in this office. I catch my reflection once more and no longer see a scared kid playing dress-up. I see myself clearly now. I am Superman.

I burst through the door and march to my desk. The rest of the group trickles out of the bathroom slowly. Mark looks at me and shakes his head. I pick up the receiver before I even sit down. I slam my finger onto the page in the open phone book and dial just as Lyle reaches forward to do the same. The ringing in the receiver echoes in my brain, bouncing off the walls of my mind like a rubber ball tossed hard by an eager child. "Hello?" A cheerful female voice answers.

"Well, hi there!" I chirp. "Is this Mrs. Moser?"

"Yes!" she says enthusiastically, "Who am I speaking to?"

"This is Mr. Bob Krulish," I say, dragging out the "u" sound in my name a little longer than usual, "and I bet you could use an account with Smith Brothers."

"Oh," she says, sounding deflated. "I thought you were someone else. I don't need a new bank account."

"Someone else?" I say. "I'm sorry about that. No, it's just me. Bob. I'm actually new here. It's my first day. I'm in the training program here at Smith Brothers. Yep. Got in without a college degree if you believe that. Well, I mean, I basically have three degrees. But I didn't actually graduate from college, even though I was more accomplished than pretty much anyone. How's your day going?"

"Well, you're chatty for a guy making a cold call," she says.

"Well, it's not about the sale, it's about the connection. That's what I always say."

"Always? I thought you said it was your first day."

I laugh way harder at her small joke than I normally would have. Lyle looks at me and gestures that I should keep her talking. I take this to mean that I should keep talking, and I do. I tell her all about Donna, student government, being a pilot, and decrypting code before she tells me she needs to go walk her dog. Just as she is about to hang up I yell, "Are you sure I can't interest you in opening an account today?"

"No thanks, Bob. Good luck." And she hangs up.

I didn't make a sale, but it was okay. I don't need sales to be the best broker Smith Brothers has ever seen.

Chapter 13

WALL STREET

I am sitting in the parking lot of the office and I can't force myself to get out of the car. I look at my watch and tell myself I'll walk inside in five minutes. I'm going to be late but I think I can sneak in without Dan noticing. My stomach is flip-flopping like a fish on a dock. My head is spinning, my breaths are quick, and my heart is pounding. I know that once I get into the office, I'll need to get on the phone and make call, after call, after call. The cocaine helps. It gives me all the energy and confidence I need to power through. But I can't afford my own, so I have to wait until it's offered. Between me and the cocaine is an endless walk to the office, flight after flight of stairs, or a long, silent elevator ride with strangers. Then there's the walk into the office itself, past everyone on the phone; sitting down at my desk; waiting for the morning meeting; going to the meeting; then the morning stare-down with the phone. Sometimes I pick up the phone and pretend to dial. Sometimes I unplug the phone and have hours of calls with no one. Sometimes I pretend to make sales, other times I pretend to be rejected. It's better than rolling the dice and hoping I don't get screamed at.

I look at my watch again and decide that I really need to go into the office. I step onto the pavement, slam the door, and glance at my car one last time. I take a moment to enjoy its familiarity. I scan the rusty tire wells, the scratches on the side, and think about the Florida plates still on the front and back. I think about how much this car has been through with my family. I can hardly believe it still runs, yet here it is, toting me to and from my dream job that I thought would make me millions. I know I'll get there. I know that piles and piles of money will be there for me soon, but for now I still have barely anything to my name. No wonder I can't make a sale. I don't own any stock myself, can't make calls to save my life, and my numbers look awful. Suddenly, a thought forms. What if I get fired? Alarm bells start ringing in my head and panic sets in. I stop walking for a moment and stomp my foot. No, I think. Not today.

I keep walking.

I try to ignore my racing thoughts and my racing heart as I finish my walk through the parking lot and into the building. I keep my head down as I make my way through the lobby, into the stairwell, up the stairs, through the office door, and straight to my desk. Mark is, of course, already at his desk behind mine. He is well groomed as always, smiling as he chats on the phone. He gives me a friendly wave. I don't wave back. I learned that Mark was hired just a few days before me and has been lagging in sales, though he has no problem making calls. I assume it's probably because he's using his calls to try and convert people. Word is, he's a Mormon, which I know only as a religion full of Bible salesmen. He seems to know what's up with Cameron and the others when we head to the bathroom. He makes it clear that he disapproves, casually cautioning me about what we're up to. I want to punch him in the face every time he speaks.

Just as I am about to take my seat, Dan walks out of his office and signals that he wants to speak with me. My throat tightens and the flopping in my stomach turns to nausea. As I start the walk to his office, I feel like I'm heading toward the gallows. I walk through the door and the smell of Dan's aftershave hits me hard. "Please sit," he says.

"Sure. Having a good morning so far?" I ask, trying to sound casual.

"Let's just get right to it, Bob. Your sales numbers are…well, I don't need to sugarcoat this, they're bad. Not everyone is born with sales in their blood. I get it."

"I know my numbers are low, sir, it's still early in the month though," I say, shifting my weight in the chair.

"Frankly, it doesn't matter what time of the month it is. Despite the tools we're giving you, your numbers at the end of the last two months were awful. But this isn't the end of the line; this is a training program after all. Remember, there's the intensive workshop in New York City next month. I just hope you can get yourself together to make at least one sale by then."

"I'll do my best," I say, perking up. I had forgotten about the intensive training in New York.

"Great. I think you'll like mixing it up with the New York guys. They're a hardworking bunch."

"Perfect, can't wait."

"I'm going to have my secretary work with you to book travel. You and Mark will leave on Monday and the rest of the guys will follow. In the meantime, let's just try to focus on sales this week, all right?"

"You got it, sir," I respond. I stand and leave the office, my body flooded with relief so intense I don't even care that I'll be stuck travelling with Mark.

Before I get to my desk, I reach over and knock Cameron's desk and point to the bathroom. He rolls his eyes, places his hand over the mouthpiece and whispers, "You need to buy your own stuff," before hanging up the phone and heading to the bathroom. I follow, knowing that Mark's eyes remain on me as I walk.

There's silence in the conference room of the hotel as Garrett wraps up the last presentation of the day. Lyle, Mark, and the others are furiously taking notes. I am staring at Garrett and the two other brokers at the front of the room. Their suits are expensive, their briefcases and shoes so glossy, the glint off the Italian leather reaches my eyes in the very back of the room. As Garrett breezes through the final slide, the lights come on and everyone begins to loosen their ties. We gather our things and Mark looks over at me and says, "Let me guess. You're going out again tonight?"

"What else would I do? Stay in the hotel room with you?"

"We could get dinner," he says as I walk away.

"Garrett!" I say, walking toward the front of the room. "Another great one today. Where you guys headed now?"

"We're going to hit up a bar or two. You in?"

I smile and say, "You know it."

The sun streams through a crack in the curtains, hitting my eyes like a laser beam. My head is pounding. My mouth and throat are dry like I've swallowed a pint of Elmer's glue. I taste cigar smoke and the remnants of whiskey. I notice there is something resting on my chest and reach up to find a half-eaten piece of pizza.

"I think he's awake," I hear Mark say. "I love you too. I'll call you tonight. Bye."

I sit up. My head feels like it's about to split in half. I toss the pizza into the trash can next to the dresser and brush the crumbs off my chest. I glance at Mark, who is now sitting cross-legged reading his Bible on his bed. I don't need his judgment right now, so I head to the bathroom for a cold shower. I step onto the tile, close the door, peel off my clothes, and step under the ice-cold water. I try to piece together what happened last night. I remember dinner with Garrett, his friends, and a few other members of the training program, drinks at a bar near the restaurant, and someone suggesting that we head to Limelight. I remember spending my per-diem on shots, I remember meeting up with a group of beautiful women and explaining to them that we were all brokers…then things get a little fuzzy. After two weeks in the New York stockbroker training program, I can say one thing's for sure. New York women love brokers.

I get out of the shower feeling better. I wrap a towel around my waist, brush my teeth, and walk out of the bathroom to get some fresh clothes.

Mark is still on his bed reading his Bible. "Good night?" he asks.

"Great night, actually."

"You know, Bob…"

"Don't start," I say, cutting him off. "Look, man, can we just skip the 'God loves you' crap today? I'm hungover and I don't want to spoil the fact that I had a great time last night and plan to repeat it tonight."

"Fine by me," he says with a smile.

"You should consider coming out sometime."

"No thanks. It's not my thing."

"Fun isn't your thing?"

"I like fun. I just don't find what you do every night fun. At all."

"You're an idiot," I say, then I head to the bathroom to change. "You know," I call, "I'm having more fun in New York than you'll have with your wife all year."

"Maybe," he says. "But at least I'm not a sinner. And I'm certainly not headed for perdition."

"Well," I say, coming out of the bathroom. "If heaven is filled with guys like you and perdition is filled with guys like me, I think I know where I'd rather be."

———

If I've learned one thing about being a stockbroker, it's that I am the man. I am the guy every man wants to be and every woman wants to be with. My numbers haven't changed much since the training in New York, but they will. I was built for this life. I am superhuman, I am all-powerful, I am everything. With my new confidence thanks to the program, I am worry-free. I burst through the door at 7 a.m. on the dot. We have our meeting, then I do a bump in the bathroom and mess around at my desk. Then I do another bump and meet a girl for lunch—whatever girl I'm dating at the time. I've learned that the key to getting rid of my phone anxiety is just to stop pressuring myself to make calls at all. So I just don't look at the phone. Ever. If someone is put through to me by accident when they choose to call one of the brokers in our office back, I use that opportunity to make a sale. That happens enough times in the month that I'm able to stay afloat, though I've never actually hit my goals. It doesn't matter, though. I am a stockbroker and it's amazing. I always thought I'd soar to amazing heights as a fighter pilot. Yet, now I'm soaring higher than I ever thought I would and I never even needed to touch a yoke.

Mark still sits behind me and still maintains his kind but judgmental view of me. Thanks to our time together in New York, we've become comfortable with our banter. He still insists I'm going to perdition and I still insist that he's a complete moron. It's a lovely friendship.

Today is Friday. It's the last day of the month and Dan has reminded each of us how far we have to go to reach our sales goals for the month. This time, he insists he wants me to get within $5,000 of hitting my goal. I know I need to land several sales today if I'm to do this but I don't care. I know the phone will ring and the problem will take care of itself. I sit at my desk and stare at the phone as everyone around me makes call after call. Lyle has read his script dozens of times already and it's barely 10 a.m. I think about reaching for the phone, but it feels like my hand is made of lead. I can't force myself to reach for it, so I don't. I stand up and pace around the office. I try to signal Cameron, then Tom, then Ryan, for our morning bathroom break but no one will budge. Everyone has their heads down trying to close sales. I sit down again and feel Mark's eyes on the back of my head. I turn around just as he says, "Great, Mrs. Pine. I look forward to you receiving your packet in the mail next week."

I want to give him the finger but I don't. I turn back to my desk instead. My throat feels tight. I stare at the phone again, willing it to ring. I miss the morning cocaine rush. I wish I had some of my own. I try to breathe through the crushing desire for the beautiful white powder. I close my eyes tightly. Just then, the phone rings. I grab it quickly. "Bob Krulish, how can I help you?" I say.

"Hi, Bob. It's Michelle Arnold from Foley's?"

"Oh, hello, Michelle. Remind me, were you interested in opening an account with us today?"

"No, silly," she says, laughing. "It's Michelle…the woman you met at Foley's, the bar, on Saturday night. Are you still up for lunch today?"

I roll my eyes and sigh. Then I perk up when I realize that although it's not a sale, it is a chance for a little fun at lunchtime. I respond, "Oh, Michelle! Yes, I'm free. Let's meet at Taco Bravo on Santa Clara. Let's say 11:30?"

"Sounds great. See you then," she says, then hangs up.

I stare at the phone, letting the excitement of margaritas overshadow the creeping anxiety that is slowly making its way through my body.

Lunch was so good. So good. Really, the perfect way to forget about the end-of-the-month stress. I ate six tacos and had just as many margaritas. Now, I feel like I'm floating on a lazy river at my desk, just watching the time pass. I think about the phone, try to will it to ring, but nothing happens. The bullpen is buzzing. I look at the clock and realize it's 3 p.m. That means our East Coast offices have already closed. I try to focus on something other than the clock. I open my desk drawer thinking I might be able to organize its contents, but there is nothing inside. I stand up and start walking around the office. I pass Dan's office and he looks at me with an eyebrow raised. I keep walking, head out of the office and down the hall. I walk until I reach the area where my mom sits. I stand at the end of the hall and look at her. For a moment, I feel like a child. I want a hug. I ignore the feeling. Shove it down.

I walk back to my office, into the bullpen, and sit back down at my desk. My heart begins to race as I look at the clock. Only five minutes have passed, but I know there is no way I can make the sales I need to without making any calls. But I can't do it. I can't hear the insults. I can't feel the rejection. It's over.

I run out of the office and into the parking lot. I fumble with my keys and open my car door. The familiar, musty smell hits me as I sit down. I hit the steering wheel with my palms over and over—the stinging causing my hands to tingle. I stare blankly ahead.

There is a knock at the window. I glance at the clock and notice that it's 5 p.m., then look at the window expecting to see my mom. Instead I see Mark holding his Bible. I want to jump out of the car and scream in his face. Instead, I roll down my window and bellow, "What?"

"Will you please come with me tomorrow?" he asks.

"I don't want to go with you to your stupid church."

"Listen, I know we don't always see eye-to-eye…"

"Correction: we never see eye-to-eye."

"Okay, that's fine. But I know you're going through something and I just want to help."

I look up at Mark. I hate him. I hate his stupid face. All I want is for him to shut up and leave me alone. But I know he never will. I sigh, then say, "I hate myself for saying this, but fine. I'll come. But when nothing happens, we're done. Okay? You don't talk about my life. I won't talk about your life. You'll leave me alone."

"I promise, if you come with me just this once, I will never, ever mention it to you again."

⁓⁓⁓

The next morning, birds are chirping and the air is cool. I walk out of my house and Mark is sitting in his idling car. I walk to the passenger side and jump in. He hands me a thermos of coffee, releases the parking brake, and begins to drive.

"You won't regret this," he says, breaking the silence.

"Something tells me I will," I respond.

I feel totally numb, completely empty. After my talk with Dan yesterday, I feel as if I've been a boiling pot of water all my life and every drop has finally evaporated, leaving me empty and scorching. I am a useless vessel.

We make the one-hour drive largely in silence, following the steady curve of San Francisco Bay. When we arrive at the towering Moscone Center, I notice every man walking toward the door is dressed like Mark. They're all in well-pressed, dark pants, white shirts, and ties. Their hair is neatly parted, their shoes polished. I look down at my light blue suit and pastel yellow shirt. I don't belong. At the doors of the center, some of the men gather with their families—children hug their legs, women hold their hands and rub their backs as they speak to one another. For a moment, I feel a surprising sense of longing.

"This way," Mark says, motioning to a staircase.

I follow and we climb the stairs and come to a crowded hallway. We duck into the auditorium, which is massive, containing about ten thousand seats. We are on the third level and I feel like I can almost touch the rafters. We slide into our seats, which are in the middle of the aisle, and look down on the stage, which seems to be a mile away. Mark leans over and says, "Listen, I'm so glad you came with me. The guy we're about to see, he will blow you away. He's one of our Apostles, Boyd K. Packer…Elder Packer. If anyone can convince you, it's him."

"We'll see about that," I say.

Within moments, the lights go down and everyone takes their seats. The crowd is eerily silent as Elder Packer walks onto the stage. My stomach flips. Just as he begins to speak, the sound system in our section booms and goes dead. There is silence, except for the murmur of Elder Packer that echoes from the lower sections. I have never heard Mark curse before, but he is swearing at the sound engineers under his breath, as if his one chance to convert the biggest sinner he knows is slipping away.

Yet, I am overcome with a feeling I can't explain. I don't dare look at Mark. I don't want to give him the satisfaction of thinking I might be feeling something positive. Although I can't hear anything, I am mesmerized. I stare at Elder Packer and feel a deep sense of admiration. Inexplicably, I am filled with the sense that I am loved. Tears well up behind my eyes. I continue to stare straight ahead. Mark is so lost in frustration over the faulty sound system that he doesn't notice that I'm feeling moved. Mark leans over and says, "I'm sorry, man."

"It's okay, don't worry about it," I say, my eyes cast downward.

Elder Packer continues to speak. I feel a swell of emotion so strong it takes my breath away. I realize as I look around that I have been endlessly seeking, striving for better, fighting to win at something, to hit some goal I've never really been able to define. Now, I'm surrounded by people who have never had to feel struggles like I have. Their paths have been unfurled for them by God himself, so they get to go through life moving from space to space like game pieces on the Candy Land board. I am simultaneously torn apart and redeemed by the simplicity of it all.

When Elder Packer finishes speaking, the crowd says, "Amen," together in unison. I exhale. Mark looks crestfallen.

We file out of the auditorium and start the journey back to my house. We drive the entire way in silence. Then, as I get out of the passenger seat and head to my front door, Mark calls out, "This counts, Bob—I'll leave you alone now."

I nod, then walk through my front door, and sit down on my couch. I realize in that moment that I don't want Mark to leave me alone. For the first time, I realize that there is another way to live and that I might just be worthy of love all on my own. Not as Bob the Answer Key, Bob the Senator, Bob the Fighter Pilot, Bob the Stockbroker. Just Bob.

Just me.

Chapter 14

BAPTISM

I t's funny how places look one way when you enter them for the first time, and after a while, they take on a whole new character. I felt that way in every house we ever lived in when I was growing up. On day one, there was always a sense of hope, walls waiting to be covered in fresh paint in colors we loved, a refrigerator waiting to be filled with food we enjoyed, beds waiting to be slept in. Then, as the days wore on, those walls were punctured by fists, the fridge was filled with leftover reminders of meals my dad had missed, and the beds were rumpled by endless nights of fitful sleep powered by worry. In the end, those houses were filled with so much sadness that they practically spit us out onto the street.

Now, sitting in Dan's office feels like sitting in one of our old homes. A place I'd once felt so much hope now feels odd and unwelcoming, as if it's somewhere I can't believe I ever thought I wanted to be. Dan stares at me and says, "You know you didn't make your numbers again this month, right?"

My face is hot. "Yes," I say.

"Listen, this job isn't for everyone. There's a lot of not so fun stuff that comes along with sales."

"I…" I start and then pause to compose myself. To my horror, tears start to stream down my face before I blurt, "I can't do it. I just can't do it. I hate the phone calls. I just can't take the rejection."

Dan looks at me with kind eyes and says, "It's okay, man. A lot of people can't handle the calls."

"Well," I say, feeling hopeful for a moment. "Maybe there's a way…"

"Let me stop you there. Unfortunately, cold calls are just a part of the job. I can't keep you on if you're not able to commit to doing them."

My mind races and for a moment, I think about trying to convince him that I can do this. I can make the calls, I can still be a stockbroker. But I know in my heart that it's a lie. I can't do it. I can't force myself to pick up the phone and risk hearing people saying awful things to me. I'm done with in the battered walls, the name-calling, and the rejection once and for all. "You're right," I say.

"I'm sorry we have to part ways," Dan says, extending his hand.

I take it and say, "Same here."

I walk out of Dan's office, and although I feel bad for myself, there is an overwhelming sense of relief just below the surface.

———※———

I am standing in a place I never thought I would. Dozens of forced visits to church on Sundays and holidays as a kid never prepared me for a moment like this one. I am standing in a baptismal font, which is basically a pool, submerged to my waist. The bishop and a group of people from the ward are standing around me, watching with sweet, loving smiles on their faces.

"Bob Krulish," Mark says, one hand wrapped around my wrists, the other in the air, "having been commissioned of Jesus Christ, I baptize you in the name of the Father and of the Son and of the Holy Ghost. Amen."

I close my eyes and ease myself backward into the water, letting it wash over me. I stand feeling completely new as if fresh from the womb.

I woke up the day after I lost my job at Smith Brothers and felt different—totally, completely different. It was as if I'd lived my entire life with goggles on and they were magically lifted. Without the pressure of work, I was free to see the value of the experience I had with Mark. I didn't even crave the sex or substances I'd indulged in almost every day for the past year. It just further proved to me that divine intervention is real. God is real. And, as much as it pained me to admit it, Mark was right. There was another way, and I wanted to take it. My full conversion took only a matter of weeks. From reading the sacred texts to finding a missionary, Mark—who was ecstatic, by the way—the process was smooth and simple.

I'd always seen life as this insane web that I had to navigate. It was this long, arduous race filled with twists and turns, and the only way to win the race was to have these major successes along the way. Whether it was straight As, the best job possible, wealth, sex with the hottest girls, there was always something to chase. But one moment in a church changed it all for me. There was only one thing that mattered. God. His love was the only thing I needed, and I had it.

Now, there is nothing to chase, there is only a path to follow. And Mormonism provides that path, offers structure, and literally hands you a playbook you can live your life by. Now, with that playbook in my hands, I feel whole for the first time in my life.

Chapter 15

UTAH

My mom stares at me blankly. She is sitting in our oversized wingback chair, her legs crossed, her hands folded on her lap. Her lips are pursed. She inhales slowly, then says, "Have you really thought this through, Bobby?"

"Of course I have," I say. "You don't have to worry about me."

"This just seems so sudden and out of the blue, picking up and moving like this is…"

"…exactly what you basically raised me to do?" I say, tilting my head.

"Fair enough. It's just…first you're going to be a senator, then you join the reserves, then you're going to be a big shot stockbroker, now this? The Mormon Church? Utah? What are you thinking?"

"I don't know," I say, crossing my arms. "Maybe all the other decisions were about my thinking—thinking I could or maybe should be something. This time it's different. This is about the opposite of thought. It's about faith."

"I'm proud of you, son," she says, leaning forward. "I want the best for you. If this is what you want to do, I'll support you."

"I want to find a wife. I want to start a family. That means meeting a Mormon girl and there's no one here for me. Girls here expect…well, they expect things to move fast. That's not for me anymore. "

"Well," she says, smiling, "I would love to have grandchildren one day soon. I'm really going to miss you."

"I'll miss you too, Mom." I slide to the end of the couch closer to her. I take her hand and look at her aging skin. I think about how it felt to comfort her after Dad left. I think about all the time I spent working alongside her at the grocery store and in our home, making sure that Rik and Kryse were raised well despite the insanity that seemed to follow us wherever we went. I was ready to leave this part of my life behind once and for all.

As I stand and walk toward my room to pack, I look back at my mom and feel a pang of guilt as she puts her head in her hands. I close my eyes, turn, and walk to my bedroom, refusing to let myself give up on what might very well be a divine future.

<hr />

Dusk falls. The jagged, red mountains look like cardboard cutouts against the deep purple sky. The courtyard is flat and dusty, bordered by willow trees whose sweeping branches hang still. Strings of twinkling lights hang above a long table set for more than fifty people. I raise my glass of lemonade and Rob clinks my glass with his. We both take a sip and one last look around before we sit. This place is paradise.

Utah is sheer perfection. I never would have imagined things working out the way they have. It makes everything I went through in the past look so petty and stupid. From the moment I arrived, I have allowed myself to be led. As soon as I pulled into town, I let Heavenly Father guide my movements. Starting with finding a place to live, I listened for prompts, navigated left, then right, then left again, and straight, until I came to an apartment complex I thought I should enter. Before my unemployment kicked in, I had next to nothing to spend. I spoke to the building manager who agreed to let me stay there for a month for $50 in a room with four other guys from the Mormon Church. I became fast friends with two of them, Kenneth, a musician, and Rob, also a musician who toured much of the year with Donny and Marie. As soon as my unemployment kicked in, Rob and I decided to head out and look for the best place we could afford.

Now, I have the life I've always dreamed of and I'm free of anxiety and fear that the happiness will disappear on me one day soon. I feel like I've achieved something real for the first time in my life. Not only that, but I feel like I deserve the happiness I feel. I have the love of Heavenly Father. I am worthy.

Rob and I sit down at a table. Other people our age are gathering, shaking hands and saying hello. It is the welcome dinner for new residents of the complex—Old Mill, the nicest in Orem. It turns out, with my unemployment from Smith Brothers, I can afford to live more comfortably in Orem than I've ever lived before. I can afford my own room in a place with comfortable, new furniture; huge windows with mountain views; a community pool and hot tub.

People begin to settle around us. I look to my left and offer a quick "Hello" to the guy who slides into the seat by my side. He introduces himself as Steve Young. I tell him I've heard about his career and congratulate him. I am beaming. I wish I had a cold beer or a cocktail, but I shake the craving. I know that alcohol isn't something I can consume anymore. Certainly not in a community like this one. Orem is nearly 98 percent Mormon, and this complex is specifically for young Mormons.

A girl settles into the seat across from me. Her brown hair is wavy, parted in the middle. Her nose and cheeks are sprinkled with freckles. She waves shyly and says, "Hey. I'm Dee."

"Bob," I say with a wave. "Nice to meet you."

"You too," she says, smiling sheepishly.

"You new here too?" I ask.

"I am, yes. I'm in 5F," she says, gesturing toward her building.

"Maybe we can go out sometime?" I say.

"I'd love that. How's next week?"

"Sounds great," I say. "I'll come by and we can figure out the details."

"See you then. I'll be back, just going to grab some food."

I watch her as she leaves and feel a sense of excitement as another girl approaches to introduce herself to me. Although I know it's wrong to entertain feelings of pride, I let this one linger. Meeting women here is going to be a breeze. I look around and feel a sense of calm knowing for sure that my future wife is among the crowd.

~~~

Instead of waiting a week, I decide to go and see Dee in 5F the very next day. I stand outside the building, pick up a pebble, count the windows, and toss it, aiming at the one I guess is hers. There is no response, so I toss three more. Soon, a woman sticks her head out the window—someone I don't recognize. She is thin with bright blond hair, blue eyes, and tanned skin. She looked around, confused, then says, "Who's there?"

"Hey, sorry!" I call, waving. "I'm Bob. I was looking for Dee. Does she live with you?"

"Yes, she does, but she's not here."

"Okay, sorry about that," I say. She is so beautiful, I blurt out, "Do you have plans today?"

She laughs and says, "Actually, I have to go return a coat at the mall. Want to come?"

"Sure!" I say. "I don't have anything going on."

"Awesome," she replies. "I'm Linda, by the way."

"Great to meet you, Linda With A Coat to Return," I say.

She bursts into laughter and says, "I'll be right down."

Less than an hour later, we are walking through the mall together. I imagine my hand brushing hers and feel a wave of butterflies so strong I feel nauseous for a moment. I stuff my hands into my pockets, then glance at Linda. Her features are angular, yet soft, with high cheekbones and a straight nose, only scooped slightly at tip. Her lips and cheeks are a matching cotton-candy shade of pink and look doll-like in contrast to her blond hair. She reminds me of Donna, but the attraction I feel to Linda is different. It's as if the boundaries Mormonism now places on my relationships has infused dating with a newfound sense of innocence. I think back on my lunchtime dates at Smith Brothers and how animalistic I was at the time. How there was nothing between my base desires and me—I wanted pleasure, whether through sex, alcohol, or cocaine, it didn't matter. Now, I realize that in seeking pleasure all that time, what I sacrificed was happiness.

I hang back and pretend to flip through racks of clothes as Linda returns her jacket. Then, we walk together through throngs of busy shoppers, all loaded down with bags and boxes. We duck into a kitchen store. Together, we browse through stacks of dishes, rows of bowls, piles of pots and pans. I pick up a set of wooden spoons, catch her attention, and place them on my head, pretending they're antennae. Then I mime putting them in my mouth like they're walrus teeth. Then I do elephant tusks and cat whiskers. Linda is laughing hard. Her cheeks have gone from pink to red and small tears are forming in the corners of her eyes. "Stop!" she squeals. "You're too much!"

"Okay, just one more," I say, laughing, doing my best reindeer impression.

"You know what? I actually do need some wooden spoons," Linda says, taking the spoons from me and walking to the counter. I follow.

The woman at the register looks at us and smiles. She punches some buttons and says, "That'll be three dollars."

"Oh, let me," I say. "I insist." I hand the cashier the three dollars and feel more like a gentleman than I ever have in my life.

The woman hands Linda the bag and says, "He's a keeper."

We walk out of the store together with the tired feeling of satisfaction that comes from a long, shared laugh. Now, as we walk, I let my hands hang at my sides. When mine brushes hers, I feel breathless for a moment, then she laces her fingers with mine. Although I met Linda mere hours ago, my hand feels at home in hers. We continue to walk that way through the mall, then out on the streets of Orem for the remainder of the afternoon.

As the sun begins to dip behind the mountains, we decide to head back to Old Mill. When we get to the complex, we pass the fountain at the front, walk through the courtyard, past the pool and hot tub, then head to my apartment. Though I know I won't allow anything physical to happen, I want to continue spending time with Linda.

When we approach my apartment door, I notice several plates sitting on the doormat. I swallow hard. I know I've been flirting with girls all over the complex, and I know a Mormon girl's way of flirting back is to bring baked goods like cookies, cakes, and brownies. Linda squeezes my hand as she notices the plates of sweet treats. I drop her hand, bend down, and pick them up. Each one has a note attached to it. I lift each note and see my name on all of them. I look at Linda, who smiles wide and says, "Don't worry. I don't mind eating food from other girls."

We walk into the apartment together laughing. We place the dishes on the kitchen counter. She sits on the counter and I stand next to her and we share the food while talking about our pasts, what we want for the future, and start to dig into things we've been through. I find myself holding back. I have allowed myself to be led here, and now something inside me says that I should refrain from telling Linda everything, and so I don't. I want her to know the good things, so I share the successes, the best parts of my childhood, and none of the hard stuff.

Finally, she leans in to kiss me. I smile as my lips press against hers. She tastes like brownies. I can tell Linda is smiling too. I put my hands on her cheeks as we open our eyes. We look at one another and, for a moment, linger at the precipice of something that feels like love.

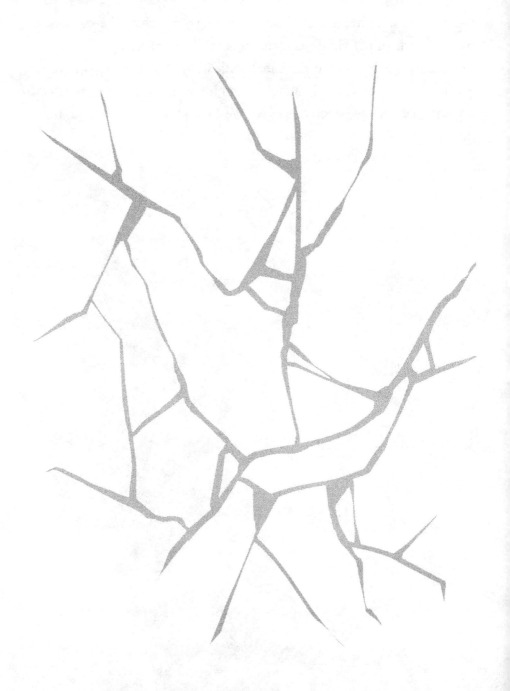

PART
III

Chapter 16

MANIC

The sun is shining, lighting the lawn in bright, golden bursts filtered through the leaves of the towering maple tree in the front yard. The kids are standing in a circle with Linda, throwing a football back and forth between them. Someone misses a pass and the ball skitters urgently away. All four of them—Logan, Amanda, Noah, and Holly—wait as Linda runs to the edge of the yard and grabs the ball. A neighbor waves as he and his family run around their yard too. The kids wave back. Linda joins the circle again, winds up, and grunts dramatically as she throws the ball to Noah as hard as she can. The kids laugh.

I look over at the grill as smoke spurts from its sides. Meat sizzles, reminding me that I am tethered to the grill and can't participate, which is typical. There is always something between them and me. I am the cameraman; the audience member; the witness.

Linda claps her hands as Amanda catches a pass from Holly, who winds up to throw a long pass to Logan. I catch Linda's eye and she holds my gaze for a moment, but her face is flat. She perks up instantly when she turns back to the kids. It's as if I am incapable of bringing her joy for even a moment. I remember the way she looked on our wedding day, just six months after we met, all laughter and smiles as I reached for her right hand. That day I received her, starry-eyed as my lawfully wedded wife, and we lived that way, passionately drinking in life for long swathes of time. I think back to her belly, the way it swelled with all four kids. The way it felt when we brought each one home, like explosive love and excitement with undercurrents of crushing pressure. Over the years, Linda built a booming career of her own as a physical therapist. What started as a career juggling dozens of clients ended in something bigger, and now she is writing a book. As Linda grew in her work, I continued to bounce from job to job, often taking on big challenges, creating large initiatives, then leaving due to drama out of my control. Whether it's ineffective leadership, faulty models, or just plain bad business, every company seems to have a weak point, and I happen to fall victim to it every time. But, just two years ago, I found a new work home in Safeco, which moved us here to Seattle, where I've put in more than my fair share of hours. Another job, another huge initiative, more time away, although I doubt anyone actually cares. I watch as Linda spikes the ball and dances, her long, spindly arms whirling and waving.

I open the grill top and prod the steaks and chicken breasts to make sure they're done. Satisfied, I take them off the heat and place them on a platter. I carry the whole thing inside and put it on the stove next to the baked potatoes and corn that are resting in bowls. I lean toward the open window over the sink and call, "Dinner!"

The kids and Linda jog toward the house. I fix myself a plate, piled high with meat, potatoes, and corn, then I pour myself a glass of lemonade from the pitcher on the counter. The screen door swings open as I gather my plate and glass.

"Yum, Dad, this looks delicious," Amanda says.

"I hope you enjoy it," I say.

Linda walks through the door last, placing the football in the corner by the doorway as the screen door slams. She looks up at me and sighs, saying only, "Again?"

"Yes," I respond.

"But it's Sunday," Noah says.

I say nothing more, just turn and walk down the hallway into the study. I sit down at the desk, drop my plate in front of me, and sip the chilly lemonade before setting the glass next to my notebook. I hear the distant scraping of chair legs on the floor, the clatter of utensils being gathered, and the clanking of plates coming off the stack one by one.

I open my desk drawer and grab the report I've been working on for months. I need to give it another once-over before I can be sure my recommendations are solid. As soon as I place my hands on the plastic folder, my throat tightens. When I open it and stare at the Safeco logo, my stomach flips. My breathing becomes shallow. My heart rate picks up.

I close my eyes and think back to the meeting where I received the assignment. We filed into the corporate conference room and sat in big, puffy leather chairs around a giant wooden table. The leadership team explained that the company was currently only serving about 20 percent of the population of drivers because they only insured individuals with zero accidents and no tickets on record. They wanted to change that, to up their offerings, and to target 95 percent instead. I knew what this meant: they wanted to go from insuring the cream of the crop to insuring the cream of the crap. They planned to roll out a program and test it out in just one market, yet they had no actual plan to unveil it. So, whoever was in charge of the market they chose would be in charge of coming up with the new products, the rating system, writing the insurance plans, and facilitating the transition. As soon as they announced that they'd start with my territory—Connecticut—I felt simultaneously excited and terrified. I knew I could create a plan that worked, but the mounting pressure felt like a stack of anvils on my shoulders.

Now, just weeks away from rolling everything out in our test market, I stare at a printed version of the plans I've written. I take a bite of corn, wipe my hands on my shorts, and open the packet. The house is quiet for the moment. I imagine one of the kids asking a blessing over the food. Relishing the silence, I read aloud, "Tier I, Plan 1. This option is best for. . ." My thoughts are interrupted by the piercing sound of laughter. Blessing is over. I take a breath and start again, "Tier I, Plan 1, This option is best for..."

"No way!" I hear Logan yell. "That one's mine!"

Amanda and Holly laugh, Linda talks over them, Noah chimes in. Their voices are muffled, but the incessant noise obliterates my concentration. I feel my face flush with anger. I inhale deeply, then start again, "Tier I, Plan 1. This option is best for..."

Linda's shrill laughter cuts the silence. I slam my fists on the desk and fly out the door and into the kitchen and before I can help it I bellow, "Everybody needs to shut up. NOW!"

No one speaks, though Logan looks like he has something to say. I shout, "You'll keep that mouth shut if you know what's good for you, son." He raises his eyebrows.

"Dad, we..." Amanda starts.

"We nothing! Go to your room!" I shout. She stands and runs out of the kitchen. I continue, "There is no we right now. It's ME. I can't get a dang thing done in this house unless you all shut up,"

"Bob, get ahold of yourself," Linda says, standing.

I am filled with rage that feels like it will spill from my eyes and burst from my ears at any moment. I hear Amanda's sobs coming from the other room and it fills me with shame, which translates immediately to anger. "Why don't you get ahold of this?" I yell at Linda, gesturing to the kids who are now huddled together on the far side of the table. Linda's eyes flicker. I am enraged. I pull my arm back and drive my fist into the wall so hard that each individual knuckle leaves a dent. "Everyone shut up and stay quiet while you eat the dinner I made," I yell. I turn and stomp toward the study, straight past Amanda sobbing in her bedroom.

I slam the door and sit down in my desk chair, which gives dramatically with my weight. I grab the chicken thigh with my right hand, which is bleeding and flecked with bits of the eggshell paint Linda and I so carefully chose. The house is silent. I look down at the paper and read aloud, "Tier I, Plan 1. This option is best for drivers with fewer than two accidents on their record."

⸺⸺⸺

I wake in the middle of the night with a start. It's as if floodlights have been flipped on and a spotlight pointed at my face, yet the room is dark and Linda is fast asleep on the other side of the bed. My heart is racing, my body drenched in cold sweat, which has soaked into the mattress, my pillow, and the sheets that cover my legs. My body feels fear in the most primal sense, but all is quiet and the house is sleepy and calm. I try to make myself get out of bed, but my legs are heavy and my chest heaves. Instead, I curl into a ball like a child. I wish for a flashlight and a comic book to bring with me under the covers, but my clammy hands are empty and trembling. I feel my heart pounding against my knees as I pull them into my chest. Thoughts speed through my mind like cars on a dark highway; images blur together like pulsing lights one after another after another. I close my eyes and pray for the morning light to cut through the darkness and rescue me from myself.

⸺⸺⸺

I stride into work the next morning as if I have it all together, but the grip I have on the handle of my briefcase gives me away. My bruised knuckles are white around the edges, nails digging into my palm as I grip the worn leather. I push the door open to see Howard, Mike, and Kevin sitting around a table in the middle of the office, playing Texas Hold 'Em. They look at me and wave. I smirk and wave back. I can't believe I'm being paid the same amount as these guys. I'm working eighteen-hour days to save the company from financial ruin and they're playing cards and eating pork rinds before 8 a.m.

I sit down in my windowless office, put my briefcase on the floor, and pull out the report. I reach forward to type my password into my computer and I feel it again, the icy grip of terror tightening around my neck. I try to steady myself by looking at the presentation, studying a bar graph, looking closely at the blocks of color, ignoring their meaning, just focusing on the colors themselves. But then I catch myself looking at the words on the x-axis. Accidents, I think. Apple, able, ambling, ambient, active, aching, airplane. As I think the word airplane my brain is filled with images of plane crashes. Wind ripping, mechanical beeping, metal tearing and twisting, masks deploying, blood spurting, smoke billowing.

There is a knock at my office door and I jump violently.

"Whoa," Kim says. "Didn't mean to scare you!"

Seeing the look on Kim's face, I realize how odd that must have seemed, so I chuckle to cover my embarrassment, then I begin laughing harder than I mean to. I catch myself, clear my throat, and say, "Sorry about that, I was lost in thought. Good weekend?"

"Yeah, thanks." He looks at me with his eyebrows raised, then continues, "Just checking in to see how close you are on finishing up those product metrics."

"I'm fine, probably just need until the end of the day."

"Well, we need it done right. Fast, but right."

"You got it, sir," I say.

He nods and turns to leave. I am alone with my thoughts again. I close my eyes trying to get out from under the feeling that I am about to die. I try to pray, but I can't string together silence in my mind long enough to detangle a prayer from my other fleeting thoughts. Instead, I give in to the fear. I let it pick me up like an invisible giant, turn me inside out, and choke the air from my lungs as I sit in silence and pretend to read.

———

When I get home the house is quiet. Linda is still awake, sitting in the dim living room on the couch. She is clutching a pencil and reading a printed version of her manuscript in the lamplight, and she looks up as I walk into the room. I know something is wrong. She doesn't wait up for me excitedly like she used to. She won't greet me with kisses and tell me about her workday and how the kids did at school, she only waits up to greet me with a criticism or a problem she can't solve on her own. I sit down next to her and turn to face her. She looks older in the low light—as if years of being by my side have depleted her. The blond hair I'd push aside to give her a kiss is now permanently swept into a ponytail, her eyes creased, mouth drawn into a disappointed slant.

"How is the project going?" she says, finally.

"Great," I respond, my throat tightening around the lie.

"I'm glad to hear that," she says, then draws a breath. "But I don't think you're doing great."

"If this is about you worrying I'll lose this job, don't go there," I say, getting ready to stand.

"No, it's about the stress you're under." She shifts uncomfortably and turns her body to face me. "You've been hard on the kids. I mean… last night was…"

My face flushes, my jaw clenches. Through my teeth I say, "Can't you even try to imagine what it feels like to be under this kind of pressure?"

"I don't want to start a fight. I just want you to be able to take a breath."

"I'll take a breath after the launch."

"Fine," she says. "Can you just try to go easier on them?"

I want to scream in her face. I want to pound my fists on the coffee table, tell her that she isn't seeing the whole picture, and that she doesn't understand how much I have to do in the coming weeks, but I don't. Instead I stand up and walk to our bedroom without uttering a word.

—————

I am sitting in the doctor's office and I want to run screaming from the building. I'm at my annual physical, and I couldn't miss the appointment because I needed a refill on my blood pressure medicine. Dr. Cooper is staring at my file, flipping back and forth between pages of lab results from my last visit. I clench my teeth and stare at her, willing her to speak so we can wrap this up. Where I really need to be is work so I can finish writing the plans and save the company from certain destruction. With that thought, my stomach flips so violently, I feel nauseous.

"Well, I didn't miss anything here, your labs are looking good," Dr. Cooper says, crossing her legs. She continues, "How have you been feeling lately?"

"I mean, I've been really stressed," I say, then add, "and it's made me feel nervous a lot of the time."

"Nervous how?" she asks, leaning back.

"I have a high-pressure project on my plate at work. A lot of people are counting on me to create something that will take the company to the next level," I respond.

"Sounds like a lot of pressure. But, tell me, in the past two weeks, how often have you felt depressed?"

I think for a minute, then respond, "All the time."

"Well, then," she says, tilting her head. "There's the problem with your nerves, Bob. It's anxiety. You're depressed."

"I am?" I ask.

"Yes, I'm quite sure you are depressed in the clinical sense of the word. It's actually quite common, nothing to worry about. There are some great medications that can really help. Have you ever heard of an SSRI?"

"No," I respond.

"Well, it's a fancy word for antidepressant. It basically corrects the chemical imbalance in your brain that's causing you to feel depressed by increasing your levels of serotonin. That pesky imbalance is likely feeding that anxiety you're feeling. Make sense?" she says, scribbling on her prescription pad. "You'll take this once a day and you'll be amazed how quickly things start to get better."

"I've only ever taken my blood pressure medication. I'm not sure what to expect."

"Well, think of this as pretty similar. The same way your blood pressure medication regulates your blood pressure, an SSRI regulates your moods," she says, tearing the prescription off the pad and handing it to me. Before I can say another word she is wishing me good luck and gathering my file before exiting the room.

⸺⸺

Linda is asleep, her head on a small stack of pillows, body curled into a loose "c." I am standing in our bathroom staring at my reflection in the mirror. My eyes are sunken, cheeks slack, brows furrowed. I try to pull my face into a smile, but it feels unnatural and looks alien. At first, the idea that I may be depressed sounded like a cop-out—a trendy way to describe the stress that comes with being a responsible human. After some thought, it feels like a label that suits me. I have forgotten what joy feels like. I don't remember relaxation. Love is a distant memory. I unscrew the cap of the prescription bottle and shake a single pill out into my hand. I hold it in my palm and stare at it for a moment. It's so small I can hardly believe that it'll do anything at all for me, but I want to be happy. I want to be present. I want to stop feeling like I my heart is going to explode. So I pop the pill into my mouth and swallow it dry.

Chapter 17

THE LAST BULLET

I stand at the stove, my shoulders shimmying to the music that streams from the radio. I tap my foot as I push the spatula under the pancake closest to me and flip it. I flip the next one, then the next, and the next until the golden underbellies of the whole batch are staring up at me. I grab a plate and stack the pancakes high on it, then turn and dance it to the table where the kids and Linda sit with their plates already piled high with bacon, eggs, and hash browns. Linda gazes at me with a soft grin and happy, wrinkly smile eyes. For the first time in a long time, I sit next to her at the table and she places her hand on my back. I continue to move my upper body, dancing to the music as I serve myself.

"Dad, you look different," Amanda says.

"Different how?" I ask.

"Your face looks more…smiley!" Noah says.

I don't want to tell him that three weeks on an antidepressant have made me feel better than I've felt in my entire life, so I say, "Well, I'd be even more happy if I had an extra pancake or THREE!" I do my best grizzly bear impression and paw at his stack of pancakes and he screeches with laughter. The growls that roll from my mouth sting my throat, but I don't stop until Noah gathers his entire stack of pancakes and retreats under the table to eat his breakfast in peace.

———

It is Sunday and I am on the pulpit gesticulating wildly. My Bible study class is packed with fifty members of the ward, and they are staring into me, enthralled. A good friend, Dixon, is in the front row with Bishop Gordon, who comes to take it all in every week. I watch as the crowd's eyes study my every move—they laugh at my jokes, which are perfectly timed, and nod in agreement as I teach through 2 Nephi 2:25. Finally, at the very end, I repeat the verse "Adam fell that men might be; and men are, that they might have joy." My face breaks into a beaming, bursting smile as I gaze into the crowd and see admiration staring back.

———

On Monday morning, I walk out to my car with purpose, barely pausing to wave at Brother Johnson who is getting into his car across the street. My briefcase swings at my side and as I reach the car, I put my water bottle on the roof. I reach for my keys, unlock the door, and fling it open before tossing my briefcase inside and getting into the driver's seat. I slam the door, rev the engine, and throw the car into reverse, stepping hard on the gas. My forgotten mug crashes to the ground and I shout, "Dang it!" before shoving the shifter into drive and stomping on the gas. I am speeding through the neighborhood; mailboxes, garden gnomes, people watering their lawns are flying by in big, booming bursts of color. I pause at stop signs and hurtle toward the stoplight at the very edge of the neighborhood. The lights turn yellow, then red, and I hang a tight right at the light, sending the car careening in front of others who approach the intersection. I speed toward the interstate serenaded by honking horns and curse words shouted out driver's-side windows.

As I pull onto the highway, I am greeted by a crimson blanket of brake lights draped across all four lanes. I drum on the steering wheel and rapidly tap my left foot. Today is launch day, launch, I think, lunch, lurch, laugh, laughter, laughable, late. I can't be late. I can't be late. L, L, L, L, what an odd letter, I think. It looks like an angle. Ninety degrees, I laugh, and laugh, and laugh. I drum on the steering wheel again, then say, "Screw it." I pull onto the shoulder and step on the gas. If an officer stops me, I imagine what I'll tell him. After all, this is an emergency. It's launch day. It's my job to save Safeco from certain destruction, and today is the day that happens. Does some bozo, low-level officer want to bring down a multimillion-dollar company? I think not. I push harder on the gas until my foot feels like it's about to hit the floorboard. Horns honk, honk, hop, hope, happiness, but I don't care. I am soaring.

Somehow, I make it all ten miles without being pulled over. I get off the highway a few exits before the office just so I can drive the rest of the way without horns bellowing in my ears. I race down the last stretch of road before I arrive at the office. I see brake lights ahead but instead of slamming on the brake, my foot sinks harder onto the gas pedal. I grit my teeth; I imagine the crunch of metal on metal. Then, instinctively, I slam on the brakes just inches before hitting the stopped car in front of me. As my body lurches forward into my seat belt, my brain flashes back to Donna—her face when she sat in the passenger seat of my dad's old Firebird. How she told me I'd fly one day. Now, look at me with a career about to take off like a fighter jet. As the car in front of me eases into a careful turn, I slam on the gas once more and throw the wheel to the left, sending my car tearing into the parking lot of Safeco. Safe, I think, solace, somber, sombrero, someone, safety, smart. Now, off to show everyone what I'm made of.

I bolt from my car, into the building, up the stairs and through the front door of the office. "What's up, freeloaders?" I say with a laugh, waving at the other product managers, who are playing cards in the bull-pen as usual. They wave and smile, shaking their heads at me.

Kim is at my office door with Mike, the president of Safeco. They follow me in and Kim says, "Today's the big day. Feeling good?"

"Feeling GREAT," I say.

"Glad to hear it." Mike smiles, then adds, "Are you sure this is going to work?"

"Sure I am," I say with a nod.

Mike narrows his eyes, then says, "Listen, remember that we're losing about a-half million dollars each and every day right now. This is the last bullet we have in the chamber. We need this to work. We need you to be sure."

"I'm as sure as I can be," I say. My heart is racing and I dab at beads of sweat on my upper lip. Kim looks at me quizzically. His expression sends shame cascading down from my face through my body—the feeling is so intense, I fear for a moment that I might be sick. Then, I notice a chunk of food in his teeth and I relax. What a dweeb. He and Mike turn to leave and I sit down, turn on my computer, and reflexively grab for my water bottle, which I suddenly remember is lying in the street somewhere outside my home.

<hr />

Days sail by, weeks, maybe months. There are numbers, metrics, data points, dollar signs, bar graphs, pie charts, and skyrocketing projections. By all accounts, the rollout is a massive success. Now it's been unveiled in every market and business is absolutely booming. I can say without hesitation that I am the man. I am sitting in a packed conference room now and Mike is going on and on about how well Safeco is doing and how we're ready to transition from growth strategies into the management phase. He's so happy with our success he is practically glowing. I know he's going to thank me. I know he'll give me the credit I deserve because I did this. It was me. Another chart pops up on the screen directly behind Mike as he talks about the unprecedented growth we've seen in almost every single market. My foot taps. I wring my hands. Say my name, I think. Bob Krulish, Bob Krulish, Bob Krulish, say it, say it, say it.

Finally, he says, "Now, I want to take a moment to thank the claims department, the underwriting department, the actuarial department, and the product department whose work has been exemplary." He pauses as the room erupts into applause, then he continues, "But, I've got to thank one person in particular, a man whose efforts have truly saved this company. Bob Krulish, we thank you for your hard work and determination."

I am so elated that I have to fight to keep myself seated. I offer a casual wave and duck my head, although every ounce of me wants to jump up, pump my fists, and scream. I feel as though I've done sixteen bumps of cocaine and drained glass after glass of dry, fiery whiskey. As the applause dies down, my face flushes. I want to run out of the room and into the street, sparks shooting from my feet as they graze the pavement. Instead, I sit quietly and pretend to listen.

When the meeting ends, I race to my office. I sit at my computer and with the company's finances in mind, I think about millions and millions and millions of dollars. The thought makes me dizzy with glee. I start searching the Internet for vacations, mansions, then the coolest car I can possibly think of. My screen glows with picture after picture of big, militaristic Hummers, some sparkling and new, others covered in splatters of mud. I click on the name of a local dealership just as Kim comes around the corner.

"Bob," he says, "that was a great meeting, and Mike was right to thank you, but I don't want you to get too relaxed. I'm not pleased with some of your numbers."

"What the heck are you talking about?" I blurt.

"Watch it," he says, as though scolding a child. "Why don't you open that report and flip to page forty-five. Connecticut's numbers are low. You got something wrong."

Then I remember. I had set the rates lower than I should have in that market and when I asked to correct the issue by raising rates 10 percent, my request was rejected. The joy I felt previously goes up in smoke, but the fiery energy remains. I am so enraged that my body feels like a volcano, filled to the tippy-top with undulating, sputtering lava. "This isn't my fault," I say, throwing my hands in the air. "And who cares anyway? My other markets are doing great."

"Who cares?" Kim repeats, his tone even more condescending now. "I do. Because I don't accept a job 70 percent well done. It's got to get sorted out ASAP."

He turns to leave and I do everything I can to keep myself seated and in control, but I slam both fists on my desk so hard that my pen cup falls over. Kim whirls around and I try not to look at him. My fists are tingling, my mind is racing, but I cast my eyes downward to avoid his gaze. He leaves.

I turn to face my computer and am met by a cherry red Hummer. I feel euphoria rush over me at the thought of sliding into the driver's seat; I imagine the smell of leather and running my hands over the newly molded plastic. I think about how well the plans are already doing and then begin to move numbers around to figure out how we can make the company even more of a profit on my near-perfect offerings. Forget Connecticut. We're going to conquer the world. I don't even care that Mike thinks we should be moving into the management phase, leaving growth in the dust. I know we should remain firmly in the growth phase for as long as we can. And I know best.

The office is dark except for my desk light, which shines a spotlight on the piece of scrap paper in front of me. It is riddled with numbers and letters, some scratched out and rewritten, some boldly traced over and over in thick layers of black Bic ink. This scrap of paper holds my formula for success—the way my million-dollar markets will soon pull in half a billion, buzzing, bubbly, basking, brilliant dollars. I lean back in my chair and stare at the paper, ogling my work.

The phone rings. I grab it and blurt, "What?" into the receiver.

"Are you coming home anytime soon?" Linda asks.

"I don't know, I'm working," I say.

There is a long pause.

"Hello?" I say.

"Holly asked me yesterday when you'll be home from your business trip. She had no idea you were even in town, Bob. You get home so late and leave so early, you're like a ghost to them these days."

"What do you want from me?" I say. Then, without warning, words begin to rush from my mouth like fanatic fans crashing the gate at a concert, pushing and shoving their way through. "I really want to know. What do you want from me? What could I possibly do to make everyone actually happy? I'm happy. I'm good. I'm about to make my company a half billion dollars. Holly's a kid. She's a kid. She's just a kid. She'll live."

"I can barely keep up with you right now," Linda replies.

I hang up. I feel nothing. I feel something. I feel everything. I don't want to go home. I want to work this plan until it's in place and I can start churning out more and more and more money. I want to spend. I want to live a delicious, opulent, lavish, luxurious life with cars, and planes, and a private island of my own. I want a rolling, roped-off, royal-looking Rolex, a briefcase made from crocodile and shoes and a belt to match. I want cashmere sweaters and a money clip and money, money, money.

I look at my watch. It's 11:30 p.m. I think about every other person who works in my office and is now at home, asleep. They're snoring away in their stupid beds and I'm here, making waves. Making a plan. Making half a billion dollars.

※

It's another day. Another day. Another day like all the other days. I woke up before the sun, brushed my teeth, tossed on my clothes, and bolted to work. There was chair swiveling, keyboard tapping, number crunching, now there is droning on and on and on.

"As you'll notice," Mike says, driving his finger into the screen that displays our most recent earnings, "things have stayed steady, which we're really pleased with."

I roll my eyes.

Mike clicks to the next slide, "You'll see here, our customer retention rates are unprecedented. And you know what that means?"

I look around the room and everyone is nodding, nodding, nodding, nodding, nodding. They're such sheep. I look at each individual and think idiot, moron, bigger idiot, bigger moron, jerk, loser, loser, loser. Kim raises his hand. Mike points to him and says, "Yes, Kim?"

"It means our management strategy is working well," Kim says.

"Oh, come on," I say, incredulous.

Mike looks at me, his eyes wide, nostrils flared, then waves his hand dismissively and says, "No. Not now, Bob."

"Here's the thing about that retention rate." I say, standing. "It's nowhere near as high as it could be, because people leave after they file claims and get their repairs done. Why? Say it with me now." I motion for everyone to speak in unison, as if they know where I'm going with this. No one speaks, so I continue, "Because the body shops we partner with do a terrible job."

The room is silent. Mike's eyes are closed and he's shaking his head. I continue, "Think about it. We get the blame for these crappy shops that don't know squat about customer care. And that's where we go wrong! You know, McDonald's, in order to ensure quality with their French fries, grows their own potatoes. They don't vendor it out. They trust themselves to achieve quality and no one else. So why don't we think like that—think about expanding? We become a company that actually does the car repairs!" I'm waving my arms now. "We don't just pay for the cars to be repaired! We create a niche. We have Safeco car repair shops whose work we can regulate and therefore stand behind." I hold for applause, and when none comes, I add, "We grow our own potatoes!"

"Stop blathering about potatoes and sit," Mike says.

I sit, suddenly filled with a stabbing pang of regret. I've given them such a great idea. They'll steal it—I know it. They'll use it, make an easy billion, maybe more, and I'll never see a dime. Why did I do that? Why did I give them that slice of genius that they didn't deserve? Why?

I stand up and storm out, head to my office, and gather my things. Kim walks after me and calls my name over, and over, and over, and over. I want to punch him in his smug, stupid face.

"What?" I shout.

"Man, you need to get a grip on yourself. Get out of here and just take a few days off," he says. Then he adds, "Please."

"Gladly," I grunt, grab my briefcase, and push past him.

I run down the stairs, out the door, and into my car. Before I know it, my tires are screeching and I'm out on the open road.

<hr/>

Sure, I took a few days away from the office, but that doesn't mean I wasn't working the whole time to figure out newer, better ways to earn Safeco more money. I'm not like Kim. I don't need to rest and recharge to be the best at this job. I'm just the best. And now I'm bolting. Bolting to the office as fast, fast, fast as I can get there. It's still dark, before dawn. I race down the highway, which is empty, inviting me to speed as fast as my car will go. I take the exit fast. I don't slow down, not even as my car feels like it will tip on the curve. I decide I won't brake until I pull into my parking spot, so I am flying, flying, curving, swerving, ripping, roaring, until I am in my space.

Inside the office, all is quiet. Something is different though. My office door is closed, but it's always, always, always open in the morning. It wouldn't be closed unless someone went in there looking for things, probably searching for plans I had, ideas, things they could use to keep pushing forward while I was gone. "HA!" I laugh. Nice try. They'd never be able to put my ideas into action without the most important thing—their missing link—my brain.

I stop when I notice that the conference room door is open and there are two HR reps sitting in there with Kim. They catch my eye and stand. It feels as though a bucket of ice water is slowly pouring out over my head, and a frigid, familiar feeling of foreboding sets in. I'm fantastic, fabulous, famous, far-out, freaky, fired. I am freaking fired.

Chapter 18

HIDING A HUMMER

pull into the Larry's Market parking lot and hang a left at the shopping carts. My eyes dart from car to car as I make sure no one I know is lurking. I see a slight woman with blond hair approaching. She is several cars away and I can't see her face, but she is wearing a pink coat and Linda has a pink coat. I duck behind the steering wheel and sneak a peek as the woman gets closer. It's not Linda. I let out a sigh of relief.

I think for a moment back to the conversation where I told her I wanted the Hummer. We were sitting outside in uncomfortable lawn chairs. She had a book propped on her chest as I explained, "I'm going to wrap it in advertisements for the company—it'll practically pay for itself!"

"Heck no," she said, her arms crossed over the book. "You're not making any money."

I couldn't explain to her that buying it would be a moneymaker, so I went to the dealership the next day and bought it without any help from her. I now commute to the Hummer in my old Camry every day and intercept bills in the mail like a boss. Once I start seeing a profit, I'll reveal it all in a fantastic "I told you so" moment.

Satisfied that the coast is clear, I turn off the Camry's engine, gather my things, and get out, locking the doors behind me. I pull a second set of keys from my pocket and click the fob, hearing a horn blow one row over. I walk quickly and begin to jog, then notice I am running. I still get butterflies when I see the Hummer in the morning light. The car is magnificent and I love it with everything I have. It is huge, imposing, militaristic—when I get to the car, I place my hand on the door, run it along the handle, then I tug. I feel the same rush of elation every time I climb in. I breathe in its scent, settle into the warm driver's seat, and let the silence cradle me. Then, I bring it to life, hear the engine growl and roar, pull out of my space, and drive.

The thing about people who are naturally intelligent is that we always land on our feet. No matter what happens, we come out stronger, better, more successful than ever before. I didn't need Safeco to make a fortune. I could do it all on my own—I could do it smarter and in a quarter of the time most working stiffs spend chained to their desks. I almost can't believe I wasted so much of my life in office after office working for unqualified boss after boss after boss.

As soon as I ran from the Safeco office on the day those chumps let me go, something shifted. Without the stress of trying to save their hides, my thinking became clearer—more focused. I realized this was my moment. It was the moment I'd been waiting for ever since I first noticed that the real estate market beginning to boom. Housing is where the money is. And I had the best way in. There was a brother-and-sister business team in my ward, Duane and Jamie, who flipped houses. They were making a killing, but to take it up a notch, they needed my mind. They needed my talent. They needed me. Barely any time went by before Duane and Jamie were paying me the same amount I was making at Safeco to help them buy and sell properties—together, we were running the company, which I will elevate to the number one spot in our market. Not only that, but Linda agreed to remortgage the house to free up cash for me to flip some properties on my own on the side. With that to spend, plus my cashed-out 401(k) from Safeco, I am speeding toward a level of wealth that most people will never see in their lifetime, because most people aren't me.

I pull out of the Larry's Market parking lot and head to an older neighborhood on the edge of town. On the passenger's seat is a stack of cardboard cylinders holding flyers I made to drum up leads. The flyers read simply "I Want to Buy Your House!" with my contact information underneath. The machine I bought to fold them is hands-down one of the best purchases I've ever made. If you ask me, two thousand dollars that will eventually earn me a million is money well spent. Linda doesn't agree, although she knows nothing about explosive business growth. Sure, she makes hundreds of thousands of dollars every year, but she'll never operate a business like the one I'm working on with franchises, partnerships, and even a TV show if I can help it. Once that happens, we'll have product lines, retail locations, and an eventual empire. But all that starts with things that Linda doesn't understand.

I zigzag across the neighborhood, tossing cylinders on doorsteps, lawns, and driveways. When I finally run out, I pull back onto the main road, realizing that if I'm going to do more, I need more paper. I drive to the nearest shopping center with an Office Max in it, pull into a spot, hop out of the car, and head inside. As soon as the doors whoosh open, I step in and inhale deeply, taking in the delicious smell of new things. I grab a cart and head to the paper section. I grab three packs of premium paper and begin to walk to the register when I see the printer section. I think about my printing quality and realize it could be taken up a notch. There is a giant poster at the end of the aisle advertising the newest laser printer to hit the market—it is sleek and black and the sample pages look crisp and perfect. I grab one of the printers and even its box feels expensive with its thick and glossy cardboard. Next to the printer is a display of things you need if you want the printer to function best, and I grab one of everything. Then I decide to take a spin down the rest of the aisles, just in case there's anything I missed. I grab a few packs of folders, a dozen packs of pens, a bulk pack of highlighters, seven black binders, a label maker, some fancy paper clips that look gold instead of the standard silver. That gives me an idea. I've been thinking we should upgrade all our supplies so our clients see what a luxury service we are. So I grab gold staples, thick, supple envelopes, and stationery to match. I yank envelope seals off the shelf, a calligraphy set, and a pack of a hundred-page protectors.

By the time I head to the register, I've filled an additional cart. As the cashier rings up my items, she glances up at me nervously and says, "Starting a business?"

"On no," I respond with a laugh. "We've been around forever. I'm a founding member. But we're about to hit the number one spot in our market. I made $50,000 just yesterday." The lie drips off my tongue like honey.

"Wow, that's awesome. I wish I could do something like that some-day," she responds.

"Well, just keep working hard," I say. "You'll get there eventually."

The beeping continues as she scans each item. After more than thirty minutes, she finishes scanning, looks at me with a smile and says, "That'll be $1,060.49."

I hand her my credit card. She scans it and the computer buzzes.

"Whoops," she says. "Declined. Let me try that again." She rubs at the magnetic strip and swipes it again. The computer buzzes again. "Hmmmm. Same thing again. Do you have another payment method I can try?" My cheeks go red and I reach for my wallet, fumbling for another card. I laugh and say, "I guess that check hasn't cleared yet! Here, try this one." I hand her another card, and the same thing happens. Then I fumble with my bank card—the one I share with Duane and Jamie—and hand it to her.

She swipes it and says, "There we go!"

Warm, buttery relief settles over me as she wrestles with the mile-long receipt, curling it into itself. I place the bags in the carts, relishing the sound of the crinkling plastic. Finally, the cashier hands me the receipt, which I quickly shove into one of the bags. I wave and leave the store, smiling from ear to ear. I picture sitting in the den and opening each package, filling my drawers with slick, shiny new things, which will get me to greatness even faster. I unload the bags into the Hummer, mentally mapping ways I can fit them all into my dinky, run-down Camry when I get back to the Larry's Market parking lot.

"It's in my hair!" Amanda yells.

"It's in mine too," Holly shrieks.

Logan, Noah, and I exchange glances as Silly String in neon pink, green, orange, and yellow swirls around their sisters. We drop the cans and pick up fresh ones, then bolt from the girls, who are running toward us. The boys break away, Noah banking left, Logan banking right. Amanda chases Noah, Holly chases Logan, and I run behind a bush to hide. The sticky summer air seeps through my clothes, causing the fabric to stick to me as if it's made of cellophane. I watch the kids as they run and I laugh to myself, feeling giddiness on the surface, but beneath it there is nothing at all. My breathing picks up, my legs feel shaky, and I curl into a ball, the bush providing cover as I try to maintain control.

I close my hand around the hand weight, turn my arm over, get into position, and curl my biceps. The weight is satisfyingly heavy and my arms burn with each measured motion. My muscles are sculpted, big, bulging. I am a well-oiled machine, training daily with Rob, a young guy from my church who is helping me realize my longtime dream of becoming a body builder. In just a few months' time, I've transformed myself into a machine at 210 pounds and just 8 percent body fat. I imagine how this hobby will turn me into a superstar. Before anyone knows it, I'll be a real estate mogul who casually slays weightlifting competitions on the weekends.

When I finish my final rep, Rob and I leave the gym and I drive him home. Then, I head back to the house, through the front door and into the kitchen for a protein shake before I shower and get to work. Linda is sitting at the table in front of her laptop and is tapping away at her phone. She puts it down and looks at me, her lips pursed.

"Busy day?" I ask.

"What's with the bags in the den?" she asks, ignoring my question.

"Nothing," I say, grabbing the protein powder from the top of the fridge. "Just stuff for work."

"So, that's it now? Dozens of pens, reams of paper, printers, that's going to be the fix now?"

"I knew you'd do that. You just don't get what it takes," I say, filling a glass with water.

"Do you get what it takes? Last week it was the folding machine, this week it's bags and bags of crap. You say you need all of this for your business, but I don't see anything happening."

"Things are happening, Linda, don't do this now," I say, stirring the powder into the water.

"Please don't act like I'm unsupportive. I've moved money around; I've made room for you to do what you want. I deserve to know what's going on."

"You deserve to know?" I shout. "After all I've done for you? All I've sacrificed for this family?"

"Yes, because I've sacrificed too." Her eyes search my face as she continues, "You have all these secret meetings with people, you come out talking about all the money you've made, but I don't see a shred of evidence that you're doing anything other than spending." She closes her laptop screen and stands.

I drain my glass and slam it down in the sink and yell, "Who do you think you are questioning my skills as a businessman? Who?"

"I think you're fooling yourself, Bob." She gathers her computer and her phone, then continues, "I think you're slowly going down. And I will not allow you to take me and the kids down with you."

I slam my fist on the counter and watch as she flinches. "You don't know a single thing about the empire I'm building."

"That's where you're wrong," she says. "I do know about it. I know because this is just another version of the thing you've been doing year after year since before we even met. But this time, it's different. There is no guarantee that you'll make back a single dollar that you've spent, and our finances can't withstand constant spending with no return on investment. You have to stop spending. I'm asking you, please, please just stop the spending for a bit until things pick up."

"What do you think this spending is for, Linda?" I roar.

"I don't know," she says—her calm tone sounds like a whisper—"and I'm starting to realize you don't either."

"Wait, back up," Mr. Erickson says, his cloudy eyes narrowing. "You want to buy my property for how much?"

"$190,000," I say with a wink. We are in his living room sitting at a card table covered in the pieces of a partially assembled one-thousand-piece puzzle of Niagara Falls.

"With all due respect," he says, his leathery hands knitted together in front of him, "that's significantly more than the last appraised value. Why on God's green earth would you make me an offer like this?"

"That's a great question," I say, giving him a sympathetic look. "We predict that this housing boom will continue to surprise us all. We've got a patented way of elevating these properties and selling them for above-market value. So, it stands to reason, we can afford to pay you above market value. Does that make sense?"

"I guess so," he says. "Sounds like a pretty great company."

"Oh it is," I respond. "And between you and me, we're heading for a TV deal. I spoke with a producer about it just last week."

"How exciting for you," he says. "Well, sir. I think you've got yourself a deal."

I smile wide and shake his hand. I think about the flip, how it'll cost just $30k, and we'll sell the place for $250k. That's $30k in my pocket today alone. Add that to the $50k on a similar deal earlier in the week and I've made $80k in the span of a few days. I want to scream this news at Linda until my face turns blue. Overjoyed, I look down, pick up a piece of the puzzle with a distinct knob, snap it into place, then say, "I'll be in touch with the contract details next week."

I bolt out the door, jog to the Hummer, and hop in. I am dizzy with excitement. I pull out my smartphone and open a search window. My brain races with ways I can find even more properties to buy and flip. I think about surveys and maps then realize I could see more from above. I type in "helicopter for sale" and wait for the results. Before I leave the driveway, I place an inquiry for a helicopter—the thing that will take our booming business to unprecedented heights.

<hr>

Logan winds up and throws the football my way. He flicks his wrist and the ball whirls toward me with such precision, I'm astonished. My hands sting as it hits my flesh. I toss it underhand back and he winds up and throws again. I can't believe his strength and precision. He's a young me. I move back and yell, "I'm going long!"

Amanda, Holly, and Noah are on the patio playing a board game with Linda. Noah turns and shouts, "Go, Daddy!" as I run backward.

"Let her rip!" I yell.

Logan pulls his arm back and launches the ball into the air. It spirals upward, climbing higher and higher until it arcs and begins to fall. The sun blinds me and I can no longer see the ball, so I stretch my arms hoping to get lucky. The ball slams down one inch from my body, startling me so violently, I stumble and fall backward. My fists ball and I sit myself up, teeth clenched. I look around at my family. Logan is frozen; the kids and Linda are silent. They stare at me, waiting. On their faces is something familiar— something I recognize but can't place. Whatever it is, it stops me. I chuckle casually, then say, "I guess I won't be drafted by the NFL this year!"

Instantly, their shoulders drop and they laugh. The sound is so beautiful, like birds singing, bells ringing, piano keys tinkling. I laugh too, harder, harder, harder until I am lying back on the ground, rolling. I jump up and shout, "Wahoo!" Then I underhand the ball back to Logan, who winds up to throw me another long packaged, purposeful, palpable, painful pass.

The house is quiet except for the murmur of Linda saying good night to the kids. The dishes are done, leftovers put away, and I am sitting in the den surrounded by the still full Office Max bags. I sit down to look for something I have since forgotten. Now, I am scrolling through my phone looking at picture after picture of helicopters. I think back to the days when I'd only enter a helicopter to decode messages—paid peanuts to waste my time decoding things that didn't even matter. Those boring brown and beige machines were nothing compared to the glossy blue, red, and silver options that stare back at me now.

There is a knock at the door and I hear Linda scurry down the hall and open it. "Oh, hi!" she says brightly. "I didn't know you were coming by! Come in!"

Then I hear Jamie's voice say, "I know, I'm so sorry we didn't call. We—"

"Is Bob here?" Duane asks, cutting Jamie off.

I stand up and scurry out of the room and meet them in the hallway. "Hey guys!" I say, shaking their hands, patting Duane on the back. "Come on in and sit! Excited about the news today?"

"Well, that's why we're here," Duane says as they each take a seat across from Linda and me.

"Yeah," Jamie says. "We just want to clarify a few things with you."

I look at Linda and gesture for her to leave. She shakes her head and says, "I'd rather stay if that's okay?"

"Of course," Duane says. "Listen, Bob, we saw the offer letter you sent out today and we really don't understand the numbers. We actually reached out to the seller and asked him to hold off on signing. That offer is way too high. We won't make a profit on the sale."

"Actually," Jamie adds, her voice shaking slightly, "we'll lose money on the deal. Like, a lot of money."

"Guys," I say with a laugh, "you're not seeing any of this clearly. $20,000 is plenty to budget for a flip like that. Then you sell for $250,000. Easy."

"But that's not right. We've been in this business for years and neither of us has ever seen a flip of that size for that little," Duane says, his face puckered.

"Duane's right," Jamie says, then pauses to chew her bottom lip. "And we can't sell for $250,000 in that neighborhood. There's just no way."

"Of course there's a way. You guys just can't see my vision, but it's there. You need to trust me." I look around the room at everyone staring at me like I'm a seven-headed alien who just stumbled from a spaceship that crash-landed in the living room.

"That's the other thing," Jamie says, looking at Duane.

"There was a big purchase yesterday—more than $1,000 from Office Max. That's a lot of money to have come out of the business account without any prior conversation."

"You're upset over a lousy $1,000 when I just made you $80,000 this week?" I say. Linda places her hand on my knee to indicate that I should keep my voice down. I ignore her and continue, "We needed supplies for all the work I'm doing to grow this thing."

"Bob, we've got to stop this," Duane says. "It's time for us to go our own way and let you go yours."

Unable to stop myself, I bellow, "Get out of my house! You're so shortsighted. You just don't get it and you couldn't leave it alone! You got your wish, kids. I'm gone."

Linda's head is in her hands as Duane and Jamie file past her. I walk with them to the door, slamming it behind them as hard as I can. A family picture falls off the wall nearby, the glass pane shattering on the floor. I want to get in my Hummer and speed toward the horizon. Instead, I go out into the garage and lift weights until my arms fail me.

Chapter 19

LOSING IT ALL

My eyes open and, for a moment, I forget where I am. I glance at my watch, sit up, and feel the tears well as it all floods back. At first, the memories lap at me softly, then they rush faster and faster and faster until I am drowning in the past. My chest heaves; my mind races. Linda's words echo in my mind, "You've never done anything for us." Her face heavy with disappointment, her hands full of bank statements, receipts, and purchase orders. Piles and piles of proof that I did nothing but spend, and take, and leech from the family. Then she points at a letter on the counter over and over. It's a bill that came from the Hummer dealership that I didn't intercept in time. And now I am alone in a crappy month-to-month rental apartment with three nearly empty rooms and a stained carpet. I hate it here so much. I hate what it represents. I hate myself for ending up here. I hate the world. I hate everyone in it. I want to leave by any means necessary. To disappear into the universe, vanish in a plume of smoke or a thick, gory splatter of blood.

I stand, drink a glass of water, and head to the bathroom. I reach for the pill container on the counter, open it, and shake a single pill out onto my hand and swallow it, wrinkling my nose as the bitterness hits the back of my throat. I look at myself in the mirror. My arm muscles are still swollen; my shoulders are bulky, my neck thick. Yet, I look unhealthy. My belly sags. My sunken eyes are framed by puffy, dark bags. My forehead is lined with thick, deep wrinkles and my hair is overgrown and graying. For a moment, I am able to focus on this body—this me. For the first time, I let myself say it out loud: "I look sick."

I hate when people hold serious meetings and mediations on couches. It's as if they're trying to soften the severity of the situation by making you sit like a child. Bishop Gordon is trying to relax his face, but he can't erase the look of concern permanently etched into his brow.

"I hear you both, I do, but Bob, you have to be fair. Linda needs space. Can you see that?"

"So that means she gets to ban me from my entire life?"

"It's not your life, this was our life, and the things you did mean that you don't get to be a part of it anymore."

I want to scream.

"I know you can't see it now, but moving you to a different ward, for now, is the best option we have," Bishop Gordon says.

Just then there is a knock at the door. It cracks open and Linda's friend Bonnie peeks in. "Lin? How about a break?"

"Sounds great." Linda jumps up and walks with purpose toward the door. When it opens, Bonnie, Mike, and three others who had previously been our friends as a couple are waiting with open arms. Linda falls into them; they put their hands on her back and guide her away. I want to run into the hallway and shove them all down. I want to ransack the building. I want to go ballistic.

Instead, I look at the bishop and say, "That's some great acting."

"Listen. This is messy," he says, shifting in his chair. "But we have to be fair, and right now, Linda and the kids are a package deal. They need to stay here. You're a friendly guy, you'll make friends quickly. Then this part will blow over and we can ease you back in."

"So," I say, pausing to bite my thumbnail, "let me review this. I have some bad luck in business. Linda gets sick of me. We go to court, she refuses to rightfully share the money we earned together. She forces me into an agreement where I get to see my kids less than OJ Simpson sees his. Then you, my friend, a man of God, think the best next step is to give her custody of our children?"

"If that's how you want to see it, I can't do anything about it. I just want peace for you both."

"She won't get away with this," I say, standing. I feel stinging in the back of my eyes and fear tears will come next, so I gather my things. "I'll agree to this, but I want you to know, this won't stick. I'm going to fight this tooth and nail. And I don't lose."

I run out into the hallway and inhale the scent of book pages and candle wax. The tears come and I take off running, wishing I could somehow run away from myself, even just for a brief time.

<hr>

Every night when the sun sets, the sorrow grows stronger. It's as if nightfall emboldens the emotions, letting them carry me where they want. Tonight is no exception as I lie on the floor, wishing I had curtains to block out the lights from the parking lot that illuminate my dingy living room. Although my apartment is bare, I have an old TV that I found in our garage. Hungry for any sound that isn't from me, I flip it on. A deep, raspy man's voice booms, "And that's why, friends, you've got to raise your standards."

The crowd cheers. The man continues, "That's it. That's all it is. You have to be willing to demand better for yourself!" The crowd goes wild. I sit up, cross my legs in front of me, and watch. The man walks back and forth on the stage, points to people in the audience, talks to them personally. He connects with them, encourages them. They light up. At first I wonder if he is a pastor, then I realize he's someone else…a motivational speaker. He is Tony Robbins.

I watch until the infomercial comes to a close. Tony says, "I want to invite each and every one of you to join me next week at my nearly sold-out seminar, 'Unleash the Power Within.' I want to see you there." He points at the camera. He is pointing to me.

I reach for a pen and paper and copy down the information, then quickly grab my phone and dial. I cradle the phone between my shoulder and my ear. The ringing drones on and on until a woman's voice answers saying, "Ticket sales, this is Billie. How can I help you?"

"I'm not sure you can help me at all, Billie, but you can sell me a ticket to see Tony next week," I say.

She laughs uncomfortably, clears her throat, and says, "Okay, let's see what I can find for you." I hear her long nails tapping on the keyboard. "How's your week going so far?"

"Awful," I say.

"Oh, it can't be that bad, sir," she says.

"Well, I've recently lost my job, my marriage, my kids, my home, my church, really everything. If I'm being honest, I'm really ready to just die."

She is silent but draws a breath.

"I hope Tony is as good as people say he is," I add with a casual laugh.

"I'm sorry," she says, now sounding muffled as if she is cupping the phone. "Listen, sir. You need to get yourself to this event. I promise you,

I felt almost the exact same way the first time I bought a ticket to see Tony. He changed my life and he'll change yours too."

"Gosh, I hope so. I'm just at the end of my rope."

"Well, hang on, baby," she says. "I've got a seat near the front with your name on it. Let's get you feeling better."

I read her my credit card number and feel lifted for a moment when it goes through. Then, I remember I have to get through seven days before the seminar feeling like a stranger in my own mind, and I suddenly no longer want to go.

Chapter 20

TONY ROBBINS

The auditorium is dim, but the energy is electric. Music is blaring, the beat catchy and quick, which causes my heart rate to pick up. I hesitate for a moment before I begin looking for my seat. I think about the elevator and the fact that I could just take it to the roof and jump off. Instead, I force myself to move forward. I walk to the front of the room clutching my ticket and slide into row C as soon as I reach it. I inch down the row, then sink into my seat next to two girls who are happily chatting. The girl closest to me turns to face me and says, "Hey there! I'm Fay."

"I'm Bob," I say with a forced smile.

"Are you so excited?" she chirps.

"Not really," I reply.

"Well, why not?" Fay asks, visibly perplexed. "Tony's seminars are amazing, you'll love it."

"I'm just"—I turn to her—"I'm at the end of my rope."

"Bob." Fay places her hand on my knee and looks into my eyes and says, "You're in the right place. Trust me."

I nod and she turns back to talk to the girl next to her.

Just then, the auditorium goes dark. People scramble to get to their seats. The music swells, lights on the stage strobe, and the audience stands and breaks into roaring cheers. Tony runs out on stage and begins to jump with the steady beat of the music. Tony spreads his arms wide, motioning for everyone to jump with him. Soon, the whole room is jumping and shouting along with the music, sending the already buzzing energy of the room rocketing. Then Tony pulls the microphone to his mouth and rasps, "Hello, everybody!"

The crowd cheers. I stare at Tony as he walks from one side of the stage to the next, high-fiving audience members; my face is flat, but my body feels the pull of the excitement that has engulfed the room.

Within a few moments, Tony slows his pace to a walk, introduces himself, then begins to talk about how we're going to make huge life changes this week. He talks about the quality of life we have versus the quality of life we deserve and how we're going to learn to make our lives better than ever. He is striding back and forth, commanding, captivating, enchanting.

Finally, he looks into the audience and calls on a young couple who are sitting in the front row. "You there," he says. "You two look like you've got some stuff going on. Why don't you tell me about it?"

"Well," the man begins, shifting in his seat, "a lot of the spark has left our marriage lately. Things are just…flat."

"Ah," Tony says. "So things are cooling off in the bedroom?"

The woman nods, then glances nervously at her husband.

"Okay, well, let me ask you two a few questions." He stands in front of them on the stage while probing into their relationship. Tony asks about their habits, their jobs, who does what in the house, and what happens between them in the bedroom. Then he says, finally, "There's your problem right there! This is a simple problem of a blurring of gender roles. See"—he gestures to the man—"you've taken on a more feminine role by taking on housekeeping duties, cooking dinners, and so on. And you," he says, pointing to the woman, "you've become more masculine as the breadwinner. Your roles are all twisted, so it's really clear why things are out of whack in the bedroom. She doesn't want to have sex with a woman, and you don't want to have sex with a man. Right?"

The couple nods and a soft chuckle rolls through the room.

"They key here," Tony says, "is pattern interruption. We've got to work together to break these patterns and make it possible for the two of you to really see one another clearly again."

Tony stands in the aisle near the couple and engages the entire audience while walking the man and woman through different techniques he uses with clients to help them change the way they've always viewed things. With each technique the couple tries, they sit closer and closer together until they are making out so heavily, I wonder if they are about to take their clothes off. Tony gestures toward the couple and the crowd breaks into thunderous applause as he yells into the microphone, "Get a room, you lovebirds!"

Tony turns from the couple, runs back to the stage, and shouts, "Okay, everyone, let's talk about something tough. Who here is depressed?" He squints as he looks out into the audience. "Don't be shy. Raise your hand if you're really depressed!"

I raise my hand and notice Fay next to me is waving her hand in the air and gesturing at me. Tony looks my way and points at me. Then he says, "You there, what's your name?"

Here we go, I think. My face feels hot as I stand and say, "Bob."

"Okay, Bob. Why are you so depressed?"

"Well, it's kind of like what you're just talking about there, with the happy couple. My wife is divorcing me and taking my kids away. She's making a lot of money and I started investing and it was taking time for me to see income. In that time, I guess I became more feminine in the relationship and she become more masculine."

"So you put your balls on the shelf?" he says, kneeling on the stage.

"Yeah," I respond, then add, "but it's a really big shelf."

The room erupts in laughter. Tony is laughing so hard, he doubles over. Adrenaline shoots from my heart, through my entire system. I feel alive, vibrant, jubilant for the first time in recent memory.

Tony dabs at his eyes, takes a breath, and says, "Is there a part of you that feels relieved about her leaving you?"

I think for a moment, then reply, "Yes."

"Because now, you can reclaim that life of yours. You can go out there and show the world who you are, then you—the real you—can win her back," he says, smiling.

"You're right, I can," I say, smiling up at him.

"Bob, I gotta be honest, you're screwing this up for me. You're supposed to be sad." The audience laughs and he adds, "Go back to being sad!"

"Well, I'm gonna do it. I'm gonna get my family back," I say, my body vibrating with joy.

"Wow! You're not the depressed, sad Bob I met a few minutes ago! Who was that guy?"

I lean forward and say into the microphone, "Little Balls Bobby."

The audience laughs, then Tony asks, "And who's this guy I'm talking to?"

I beam and say, "Big Balls Bob!"

The audience breaks into cheers and applause so loud, I feel as though the energy could lift me out of my seat and over the throngs of screaming fans. I am lightning. I am thunder. I am Big Balls Bob. I am back.

Tony talks for several more hours. There are breaks, other audience members called out, other people healed, and every so often, Tony checks in on me. He gestures and a cameraman runs over to capture my response. I'm always there, poised with a big, flashy smile.

Now, Tony is finishing up a segment about the big event we're about to participate in: walking on hot coals. He says, "Now, when we go out there, we're going to do something you've never done before. Something you've only dreamt of. You're going to…"

"Conquer fears?" I shout, interrupting Tony mid-sentence.

"Big Balls Bob?!" he says, without missing a beat. "Look at that guy! Look at the change in him!" The crowd applauds and he continues, "That's right. We're going to storm across those coals and conquer every last fear we're hanging on to."

Tony winks in my daring, dopey, dandy direction and I wink back. I am ready to charge across the coals like they're nothing. I imagine myself stopping in the middle of the pit, reaching down, and grabbing handfuls of scorching, screaming, scalding, scarlet coals and shoving them into my mouth like pieces of popcorn.

On Tony's command, we stand and move toward the exit. I walk through the crowd with purpose, hands patting my back, reaching to offer handshakes and high fives as I approach the parking lot like the star player headed to the field. I walk out to the parking lot, taking in the cold night air as I walk, my chest puffed, eyes forward, waving at folks I've come to know. The audience loves me just as much as they love Tony, if not more. I can't imagine how he'd have done this whole thing without me.

I can smell the smoke as I approach the beds. I am so ready, I want to charge, but a woman in a headset comes up beside me and stops me, saying, "Hey, Bob? I need you to come with me for a minute."

"Okay," I say, feeling like royalty being whisked away. We walk for several minutes before we reach a thick metal door to the backstage area. She punches a code into a panel, then pushes the door open. There, sitting on a plush chair, is Tony Robbins.

"Look who I brought!" the woman says. "It's Big Balls Bob!"

"Bobby!" Tony says, standing up. "Great to see you!"

"Hey, man!" I say, offering the firmest handshake I can muster.

"Listen," he says, "I'm so glad you came to the seminar. I can see the changes in you. I know you're gonna do great things." He motions for me to walk with him and says, "You're hitting the coals with me tonight, man. Let's go!"

I say nothing, but I feel as though my smile could crack the corners of my mouth. I walk with Tony; throngs of people gather in the parking lot to watch us make our way to his VIP bed of coals. The crowd cheers as we approach the glowing bed. He yells over the crowd's murmurs, "You are strong! You are powerful!" The crowd's energy becomes my energy and I kick my shoes to the side and begin hopping from foot to foot, jogging in place. I follow Tony's lead, beating my chest, shouting into the sky. I am almighty. I am powerful. I am the earth, the sun, the stars, the ocean, I am the earth's explosive core. I look at Tony once more and he puts his hands on my shoulders and whispers in my ear, "Go get 'em, Bob." As if sparked by his words, I take off, walking quickly but methodically, so I don't kick up coals. As I walk, the crowd goes wild, cheering, screaming my name. I become fire. When I reach the end of the walk, people are ready, spraying my feet with a hose, but I feel no pain.

———

For the rest of the conference, I am treated like royalty. Tony's team gave me a name tag that says Big Balls Bob, which I've worn proudly ever since they peeled off its backing and stuck it to my sweater. Ever since my coal walk with Tony, there has been a cameraman dedicated to catching my reactions while Tony is on stage. Every few hours, Tony would catch sight of my smiling face on the big screen and say to the audience, "Look at that smile on Big Balls Bob!" and they'd break into applause. I feel astonished at the comfort brought to me by this small measure of fame. For the first time, with all eyes on me and applause rolling toward me like wind in a field of wheat, I am somewhere that feels like home.

At one point, while we were waiting for a segment to begin, someone came by, patted me on the back, offered congratulations, handed me his business card, and asked for mine too. When he walked away, I looked over at Fay, who was gawking at the card in my hand.

"What?" I asked.

"Are you kidding? That was Dr. Oz!" I had no idea who Dr. Oz was, but I tucked his card into my wallet for safekeeping.

In that moment, I closed my eyes and let the amazing, amplifying, absolutely awesome adrenaline course through my veins. I think back on the way I entered the building just two days earlier and can't even relate to myself in that state. I imagine myself running up the stairs, bursting through the door on the roof, sprinting toward the edge, and flinging myself off. Only, now, instead of falling, I picture myself taking flight.

Chapter 21

DR. OZ

"Okay, folks," I say into the camera, "until I see you again, live with energy." I pause for a moment, then lean forward and hit the red button to stop the recording. I feel better than ever. I've learned so much from Tony Robbins that I know I'll be the best Bob Krulish I can ever be thanks to him. In just a few days, I'll finish compiling my videos and start getting them out to my throngs of hungry fans, capitalizing on the fame of Big Balls Bob. The videos will go viral, I'll start selling tickets to my master class, and before I know it, I'll be rolling in cash and Linda will be begging for me to come back to her. The path is so clear, I can't believe I didn't see it before.

It has been an incredible couple of weeks since I left the seminar. I am off all my medications, am running miles and miles each day, am drinking a ton of water, and producing content that is so stellar, it will change the world. I've already emailed everyone whose card I received at the seminar, including Dr. Oz, who I now know to be hugely famous. I can't believe that I was going to kill myself just four weeks ago, and now all I want to do is thrive.

I ran out of money before I was able to get the last piece of audio equipment I needed so I sold the few pieces of furniture I had from our old home and some tools I had from flipping houses. Although my apartment is empty, it's ended up working in my favor. I've created a mini studio with state-of-the-art video equipment I purchased with the last of my Safeco 401(k), complete with a green screen and lighting. I also bought a new wardrobe to perfect my signature style, which is sporty but polished. I've got energy, passion, and drive so pure that it basically bursts off the screen. I can't wait to see the material I just shot, so I fumble for the cord to connect my camera to my laptop.

Once I find the cord, I open my computer and start to plug in the camera when my phone rings with a number I don't recognize. I answer and a cheery, female voice says, "Hello, Bob?"

"Yes, who's calling?" I respond.

"My name is Erin. I'm a producer with a radio show hosted by Dr. Oz and his wife, Lisa. I've been asked to reach out to see if you'd like to come on the show sometime soon. They would love to talk to you about your experience with Tony Robbins. Are you in?" A rush of excitement floods my body—it is so strong; I can barely see straight for a minute.

"Sure," I say, trying to sound casual.

"Great," she says, then talks to me about a date and time, how to get to the studio, what the process will be like, and more.

When we hang up, I feel like a firework bursting into a thousand bits of flaming glitter. I am punching the air, hooting and hollering. I think about how I'll plug my videos, how his listeners will be clamoring for my content, and the millions of dollars just cascading my way. Within minutes, I am fumbling for my last good credit card, booking a ticket to New York City.

The day before the show's taping, I wake up and nearly jump out of bed. At dawn, I race to Pike Place Market and buy a pound each of salmon and halibut, which they put in a box on dry ice, and place the whole thing in a paper bag with handles. Then, I hop into a cab and bolt to the airport where I scurry through security, to my gate, and onto a plane, which hurtles down the runway and catapults me to the Big Apple as the sun begins to rise.

The next morning, I wake up in the hotel and take an ice-cold shower, dance into my clothes, and shimmy as I check my email. There is a note from Linda with the subject line Ongoing Financial Relationship. Normally, an email like that would put me in bed for three days, but today I see it and I feel nothing. It's as if learning my own value has taken away all her power over me. I am incredible, invincible, important, impeccable, and she's just plain old Linda.

I gather my things, pull the fish from the freezer, place it back in its paper bag, and head out of my hotel room. I burst into the hallway that smells like new carpet and chlorine, head down the elevator, and walk quickly through the lobby and onto the street. I make my way through Rockefeller Plaza with ease, navigating the grid of the city's streets like a pro. I close my eyes and inhale the scent of commerce, mixed with exhaust from the countless buses and street meat. My body remembers how it felt to be here as a young stockbroker and butterflies come to life in my stomach. As I get to the building, my cell phone rings. It's my landlord calling for the sixth time in two days. I clear the call. I'll pay my rent in the next couple days when my settlement with Linda comes through.

I sign in at the front desk, receive a visitor pass, and head into the elevator bank. I step into the first one that opens, press 12, and my belly drops as the elevator zooms up. As soon as it stops, the doors glide open and I am in a cavernous hallway lined with glass windows. When I look closely, I realize every room is where a different radio show is taping. Radio, I think, rational, radical, rapid, ranging, rambling.

The hallway is lined with windows that look into studio after studio. As I reach the green room, I casually glance to my right and notice that there is a door to the only windowless studio on the floor: the one that belongs to Howard Stern. I want to bang on the walls and yell, "Are you in there, Howard?!" but I play it cool and walk by as if I've been this close to a million superstars in my life. I walk into the green room still clutching the box of frozen fish. Within seconds of me entering, the producer I'd spoken to comes into the room and says, "Mr. Krulish?"

"That's me!" I respond.

"Great to meet you in person," she says with a smile. "Come on back."

I follow her swinging ponytail down the hall and to the glass door of the studio. I walk in behind her, she pulls the chair out for me, points out the switch on my microphone. "Would you like some coffee?" she asks.

"I'd love a water," I say, then watch her leave. I sit and place the box of fish on the floor between my feet.

"Big Balls Bob!" Dr. Oz says as he and his wife, Lisa, finish their conversation and stand. "Good to see you again!"

"Bob, lovely to meet you," Lisa says. "I hope you don't mind if I just call you Bob?"

"Oh no, just Bob is great," I say, shaking their hands before they take their seats across from me again. The girl with the swinging ponytail comes back in with a bottle of water and a full-sized candy bar and places them in front of me.

"Perfect. Well, then," Lisa says. "Did anyone fill you in on what we're doing here today?"

"You guys just want to talk about my experience at the seminar? Maybe what's happened since?" I say.

"That's exactly right. We'll be live, so just try to be honest, keep it clean, and share your experience."

Before I know it, a sign above our heads that says "on air" is illuminated and I'm talking about my experience learning from Tony. I'm talking about Linda, the kids, how I wanted to kill myself. I tell them how much better I'm doing, how things are coming together, how the settlement will come through and my videos are coming together, and how I'm going to be rich in a matter of days. How I've lost weight and am drinking water and no longer have a need for any medication at all. They engage me expertly, gently prompting me to continue speaking when I slow down, nudging me for more information when they need it. As I speak, I watch as they drink in all I have to say. They are wide-eyed, smiling, and laughing. They love me.

Finally, the interview draws to a close. Dr. Oz says, "Any final thoughts, Bob?"

"Just that if anyone out there is feeling hopeless or sad, please do yourself a favor and get yourself to a seminar.

The sign clicks off and we shake hands once more. Then I reach down, grab the bag of fish, hand it to Lisa, and say with a wink, "I hope you all enjoy this. I got this for you fresh from the dock yesterday morning. It's on dry ice!"

"Wow, what a gesture," Dr. Oz says. "Thank you so much."

"We can't wait to see what you do for the world, Bob," Lisa says.

Then I turn to leave, feeling like I'm walking on air.

Chapter 22

IT DOESN'T ADD UP

Something is wrong. Something is wrong. Something is wrong with me. I returned from New York City with so much stamina, I knew I would conquer the world. I edited my tapes, again, and again, and again. They were perfectly timed and polished to perfection, ready to hit the Internet and make a splash. Then I sat to watch them one last time, and instead of feeling fiery joy, I felt flat. I felt nothing. I felt bored by myself.

After six more watches, I knew they needed to be fixed, but I felt completely and utterly incapable of figuring out how. I couldn't edit them further. I couldn't fix what was broken, mostly because I couldn't identify any single thing that was wrong, yet nothing about the videos, or anything, felt right. My inbox was filled with responses to all the emails I had sent about my business taking off. Previous investors were reaching out wanting to revisit relationships now that I had told them of my healing, yet I was unable to respond. In fact, I was unable to get myself to do anything more than what was absolutely necessary for my survival. I could breathe. I could ingest small amounts of food that were already in reach—crackers, cookies, candy. I could drag myself to the bathroom. Yet, even those things took hours to work up to. I spent nearly all of my time sunken into the couch I had dragged inside from the curb. It had been soaking in the rain for days at a time and is still damp and musty smelling, but it is mine now, and I don't care.

Everything started to unravel when emails from Linda came more frequently. Then her lawyer started calling, then they served me with papers. I went to the courthouse on a break from editing where I sat and they told me that I would not be receiving my settlement from Linda. Instead of the million dollars I thought I'd get, I would receive a small portion of what she claimed we had in the bank. She produced a certificate of deposit for $100,000 and claimed that plus the $700,000 equity on our house was all we had and that I was entitled to half of it. I thought about the videos, about Tony, about how rich I was about to become, and the money meant nothing to me in the moment. Instead of thinking and arguing, I said, "If that's all there is, I want you to have enough to support the kids." I then offered to let her take $700,000 and walk away only with $100,000 and a commitment to pay $50,000 toward the debt that was in my name. Although something felt off about what Linda claimed we had, I wasn't able to hang on to that nagging feeling. My racing thoughts of fame and fortune were just too strong. So, I signed the papers.

Now, from the couch, the only things I can see clearly are my failures and the eviction notices that keep sliding under my door. I can't believe I let myself sign those papers. The number that meant so little to me in the moment is now the only thing I can think about. There's no way that's all we had in the bank. How could I be so stupid?

In the dull void that is my apartment, my deterioration is palpable. My body periodically shakes violently, my hands are clammy, my limbs feel heavy. It's as if someone has force-fed me cement. If I jumped into a river right now, I would sink to the bottom and be sucked into the silt until fish ate my flesh and I was bone. And then it hits me again. I want to be bone. I want to be dust. I want to be forgotten, like an old shoe on the side of the road. My mind reaches for it, digs through my mental files for all the ideas I once had about creative ways to take my own life. I sink into the mold-covered couch and dream of death by any means necessary.

—⁂—

Time passes. I don't know how much, but it's three more eviction notices' worth. There is banging at my door. I think it's the cops so I don't want to answer, but I imagine them kicking the door down and finding me rotting in my underwear and I can't bear the shame. I grab the blanket that is draped over the couch, which is really an old, stained towel, and I wrap it around my shoulders. I open the door to see Dixon and Bishop Johns, the bishop of my new ward. I look down at the floor. I want to shrink away, to melt, to fade, but I stand there. I step aside and let them in, close the door behind them, and lead them to the couch where I sit.

"How did all this happen?" Dixon asks, his face dripping in pity that stabs at my guts.

"Linda took everything," I manage to say.

"We've been praying," Bishop Johns starts, but he recoils quickly as he sees my body contort. My eyes are fixed on the wall behind them, my muscles contract, and I fall back against the cushions, shaking, jerking, convulsing. They move me to the floor, push the couch to the side, and Dixon holds my head until my body stops moving and I go limp.

My eyes flicker and I see them standing above me. I curl into a ball, roll to my side, and cry thick, hot tears.

"I'm calling your doctor," Dixon says, taking my phone from the couch as he stands. Before he leaves the room he kneels again and asks, "Are you taking any medicines now?"

I shake my head and whisper, "Not anymore."

Dixon leaves the room and Bishop Johns stays with me, his hand on my back, praying over me. He says, "I'm reminded now of Doctrine and Covenants 121, which says, 'My son, peace be unto thy soul; thine adversity and thine afflictions shall be but a small moment; And then, if thou endure it well, God shall exalt thee on high; thou shalt triumph over all thy foes.' You will get through this, Bob."

I say nothing, but I continue to cry. My breath catches dramatically as I try to inhale. The room is quiet, but I hear Dixon speaking in a low voice into the phone in the kitchen. He says, "Yes, I think it could be a nervous breakdown. His wife left him with nothing; his life is in shambles. No, he says he doesn't take anything. Yes. I will." I hear his footsteps coming toward me, then he kneels and says, "Okay, we've got some medication being called into the pharmacy across the street. I'll go get it and we'll get you feeling better."

Dixon leaves and Bishop Johns helps me into the bedroom. I roll onto the mattress that sits on the floor and curl into a ball again. The bishop paces the room until Dixon comes back with a bottle of pills and a bag of groceries. He motions to the bishop and whispers something to him. I strain, but all I hear is "…if he stopped them too fast, that could have done it."

He hands me a bottle of water, then puts packs of protein bars and other essentials next to the bed. I open the bottle and swallow a pill and within minutes, my thoughts are swimming, floating weightless through time and space until I close my eyes and let sleep drag me into the abyss.

───※───

My life has become one endless, ambling walk. I wake up in the morning, splash water on my face, pull on clothing of some kind, and leave. Sometimes I walk to meet with Bishop Johns. Sometimes

I have meals with Dixon or pace the park for hours, usually thinking about the kids and how to get back to seeing them more regularly. On the days when I couldn't stop thinking about the kids, I'd walk until long after the sun set, hardly noticing the big, pus-filled blisters forming on my heels.

I used to love to drive, but that's not an option now. My Hummer is long gone. It's okay that I am forced to walk now. I think as I walk, but the medication Dixon got me keeps me dopey. I get angry, I get sad, but these feelings are dulled and muted like a television blaring a mile away. I plan to appeal the court's decision. I plan to get my life back, to get the money I deserve from Linda, but I can't do anything to move things along faster. The owner of my apartment has been understanding; the eviction notices have stopped coming, and I have promised her to pay in full as soon as I get my money. For now, I pace the town for hours, walking slowly to fill my time. I wish days away, will them to pass, but they ooze by like molasses.

I have let the church care for me in ways my mother never did. I let them baby me, buy me groceries, and even send me to psychotherapy, which is where I am heading today, the one day I have somewhere to be. I've been walking for close to two hours and have switched from bus, to bus, to bus. Now I am entering Dr. Shaw's office to sit in her waiting room and listen to the whirring of sound machines that drown out patients' whispered secrets. She opens the door and greets me in the same familiar way: "Hello there, friend."

I stand and walk through the door, unable to muster a greeting. I slump onto the leather chair in front of her desk and sigh. She sits at her desk, her brown curly hair framing her face. She adjusts her glasses and looks at me before saying, "Any better at all today?"

"No," I respond.

She pauses, leaving space for me to elaborate. When I say nothing she says, "Listen, sometimes offering a diagnosis can be problematic.

Believe it or not, very often, psychiatrists will try to shepherd patients to the right treatment without naming what they have."

I nod, pretending to understand.

"I'm beginning to wonder if it might actually help you, rather than working through what's been going on in an abstract sense, if it might not be better to get you some solid answers."

I nod, enthusiastically this time, then say, "My doctor told me a while ago that I have depression."

She flinches, then says, "I know, I remember you telling me that. And I wanted to offer some insight there. When I look at the whole picture of Bob Krulish, take your whole story into account, depression is not what I see."

"Okay," I say. "Then what do you see?"

"Have you ever heard of bipolar disorder?"

I shake my head.

"So you don't know what it is?"

I shake my head.

"Listen, I'm not an expert in bipolar, but I happen to know someone who is. Instead of talking you through this, I want to advocate for you and get you an appointment with him. Please, please, Bob. When I get you this appointment, I need you to show up. This doctor is highly sought-after and will not take kindly to you missing your session."

"I will, I promise," I say.

We talk a little longer, but I am completely distracted by the notion that there could be a reason that all of this is happening to me. There could be a name to what I've always just thought was my rhythm. As I stand to leave, I am struck by something so powerful, it takes my breath away. It is an image of my father, standing in the yard at night shirtless, screaming at the sky. For the first time, I think about him and am struck by a feeling of something so new it grips my throat, clamps my windpipe, and stirs my guts. It is empathy.

Chapter 23

SEARCHING FOR NORTHUP WAY

Today is the day. Today is the day I get answers. It's been two weeks since my meeting with Dr. Shaw when she suggested I see a specialist. That night, I flushed the sedatives I was taking down the toilet. With them out of my system, my emotions have felt sharp, pointy, hard to control. But I want to feel them. I want to soak in the crazy, because it is mine, it is me. I want to revel in it, to know it, to learn its every corner before I meet with Dr. Palmer.

Ever since Dr. Shaw got me thinking about it, I've felt burdened and betrayed by the way my own brain works—or doesn't. It's like a child's puzzle—most of the colorful pieces jammed haphazardly into the wrong spots. I know a few pieces are snug where they should be. But the rest are just plain wrong. I am weighed down, sucked to the earth's crust by what feels like quadruple gravity. It's almost as if an elephant is resting on my back, allowing itself to relax its full weight on my flattening body. No one in my life believes that this is real. They think I'm a total loser, a terrible husband, an incapable father. They think I make irresponsible decisions, say whatever I want, and explode into fits of rage on purpose. They think I somehow enjoy losing everything I've got. But the joke is on every single one of them. Because today is the day I get proof that my actions aren't always my own.

I know I have to take the bus, and I'll go from bus 269 Overlake to the 221 Eastgate and get off near Northup Way. Then, I have to get off the bus and head east onto Northup Way and walk until I come to the building marked 2820. It'll be a tall glass building with slick sliding doors, and I can already imagine the air conditioning hitting me in the face when they glide open. The elevator will smell like cologne, and the doctor will look me in the eye with the hint of pity I've come to hate.

269, I think. 9, nine, n, notice, naptime, no, no way, normal, never…

I don't need anyone to feel bad for me—as if I'm someone who doesn't see himself clearly. I know I'm crazy. I just want to know what kind of crazy I am.

It's 6 a.m. My appointment is at 8:40, and the office is an hour away. I want to give myself plenty of time in case I get lost or hit by a car, or a bus, or by a kid riding a bike. Anything is possible, even an alien abduction. They exist—they have to. This universe is just too big for them not to. But it doesn't matter; I'll evade them in the extra time I have. I must be on time and I will be on time. This doctor has a reputation. He won't see any patient who is even a minute late. I respect a guy like that, but it's already getting on my nerves too. Why would he choose to make people like me feel more anxious? Does he get sick pleasure in making us writhe in our own skins?

As soon as the thought crosses my mind, I wonder if it's true. Those jerks. All of them. All three of them. They were once such great friends to Linda and me. And now, they're great friends of Linda's, backing her every move as she lies and cheats and hoards what we earned together.

They rub her back. They shield her from me at church, and they never miss a chance to point out every asinine thing I've done to anyone who will listen. As if I need to feel more shame. As if I need to hate myself more for the things I've done—for the person I've become. And they seem to love it, seeing me dissolve in the acidic soup that has become my marriage.

The 269 pulls up right on time, and I climb the steps looking straight at the driver. I am holding something. I think it is money, but it may be a token or just some round piece of metal like a bottle cap. Suddenly, I can't remember what to do with it. My brain controls my eyes, which look at my hands, which suddenly release what I'm holding in the driver's direction. He looks at me like I've lost my mind but nods for me to sit, and I do.

I am suddenly overcome with the irony of riding this bus. It is the one I had once almost stepped in front of to end it all. That was just a few weeks ago. Now, as the bus lurches forward, I imagine it crushing my body, crunching my bones. I would have done it. It wasn't an epiphany about my life that stopped me. It was my fear of ruining the bus driver's life—the one who would be forced to take my life. My therapist pointed that out, and I knew instantly she was right. It wasn't fair for me to check out and pass my mental demons to someone else. If I ever were going to "check out" it would have to be by my own hands.

Staring at my feet, I repeat my next step to myself in a whisper, "Get off at the third stop and wait for the 221." 221, I think, one, O, octopus, opulence, wealth, wealthy, week, weekly, weekend… My mind continues this cycle until it finds its way back to octopus, just as the bus stops for a third time.

As I reach up to pull the signal cord, I notice I am sweating hard through my red T-shirt and the man in the seat across is staring at me intently. He looks like the kind of guy who has a wife who hasn't thrown him out of the house. He probably has kids who he throws a football with and reads bedtime stories to. Of course, I want to be extraordinary in every way, but mentally, I just want to be normal like this jackass. Normal. N, I think, N, Nancy, notebook, notes to friends, friends, fables, falsehoods, lies, laboring, lamenting… I pull the cord hard and the bus comes to an abrupt stop before my brain makes it back to n.

269 to 221, 2820, I think.

That's my path. My path back to sanity, back to real life, back into my house, back to a place where there is some semblance of hope.

I run to the door as it opens with a screech and jump off the steps into the hot summer air. Soon, the 221 arrives. This time, when I make it through the heavy, hot exhaust and reach the top of the steps, I remember to put my coin into the slot. I try to avoid eye contact while finding a seat beneath an air vent. I need to let the cool air hit me in the face. I focus on one word. Stop. Stop. Stop. Stop. I tell my brain, this is my safe word. Stop. I want out of these maddening thought circles. Now. My mind feels compelled—pushed like an elephant is leaning against it—it reaches for the c in circle and wants to begin the cycle all over again.

My brain strains for the c, and I can't suppress the word cash that screams at me. I push back. I try to say Stop, yet my brain flashes to the moment when I signed the settlement. 221, cash, court, and I remember the way I signed the documents so casually, like I was buying Girl Scout Cookies. 221, cash, court, church, and I feel the heat of anger rising in my face. Being treated like a pariah enrages me. I am not the garbage person in this situation. I squeeze my fists so tightly closed that my nails dig into my skin. I want to scream and shatter every window on this bus, but I can't. I can't. I can't.

C, c, c…

I realize I am giving into the crushing pressure, and I push back hard. I'm pushing with all I've got, but I'm being bested by the weight of this beast. Stop! I yell in my mind. FREAKING STOP! Stop. I'm at my stop!

"STOP!" I yell, pulling the cord too forcefully. All eyes are on me as I check my watch and run to the door. It's 7:00.

I hop off the C still struggling to control the obsessive urge to let the thoughts chase one another. And now, I'm climbing onto the F, and I feel like a genius that my mind recalls what to do with my coin. I sit down knowing I only have to go three more stops. Then, I'll make the walk down Northup toward the person who may decide my fate.

F, fate, fight… my brain begins. I clench my eyes closed and grit my teeth, pushing back on the elephant with every ounce of strength I have. Imagining the look on Linda's face when I hand her the proof that my actions aren't completely my own gives me the tiniest bit of strength. She'll look me in the eyes. She'll feel bad. Maybe she'll even cry. She'll let me come home.

Staring out the window, I see cars whiz past. Suddenly, my mind breaks against the weight of the elephant. My subconscious chases each car like a dog with a death wish. Blue, blueberries, blue whales, blues, rhythm and blues. Yellow, yard, yarn, sweater, hot, heat. Red, wagon, wagon wheel, wheels on the bus, BUS "STOP THE BUS!" I yell, realizing that we're about to move past my stop. Once again, everyone turns to stare as I hurl myself onto the pavement on Northup, my knees taking the brunt of my weight as I land.

269 to 221 to 2820. Okay, I know I need to turn right and walk until I see building 2820, so I turn and start walking. And I walk. And I walk. And I walk. When I look at my watch, it seems like the minutes are passing in increments of ten, and now it's seven o'clock on the dot. A man jogs by a little too close to me, and his shoulder catches mine hard enough to knock me back a step.

"Watch yourself, guy," he mutters, his nylon shorts clinging to his chicken legs.

I want to scream at him and at the sky and at God, but I don't have time for that crap. I'm looking all around me now and nothing is making sense. The buildings are all the same shade of monochrome gray, and none of them sticks out as the one I need. Plus, the numbers on the Northup Way buildings aren't even close to 2820. They are much smaller and as I continue to run down the street, the numbers are getting smaller. Perfect. I'm going in the wrong direction.

I pause and try to take a deep breath. The air stops in my throat, and I need to lean against something. I jog to a lamppost and push my back against it until the ridges dig into my spine. Thoughts bounce around my brain like a spiked volleyball in a glass case. I look at my watch. 7:10.

Ten, T, tennis, tennis ball, table, trunk, truth…

Okay.

Truth.

I am lost.

I will miss my appointment.

The chance of holding proof in my hands will evaporate.

Then I will have to go home and kill myself.

Great.

A chill starts at the crown of my head and slowly drips over my entire body. I look up and try to take a methodical approach. I shove my thoughts aside. It is an arduous task. The elephant has become angrier now—I can feel his determination. I am breathless. STOP!

Okay. I am outside building 880. I'm really far.

I walk one hundred feet farther in the direction I feel is correct. I close my eyes and raise my head, praying to see 409. Yet, now, I am at building 590, and the street name has changed to NE 20th St. I think I might drop dead. I want to ball my fists and punch away at the burning cement beneath my feet.

I make a snap decision, turn around, and start running in the direction I just came from. It is 7:15, and I need a miracle. I am running fast, up and down this street for nearly an hour, hoping that by running it will somehow change its name back to Northup. Now I am aiming for a person in a fluorescent vest working on the road. She is a short, jolly-looking black woman with bouncy curls that shine in the bright sunlight.

I run up to her and yell, "Hey! Lady! Do you know where 2820 Northup Way is? What way do I go to get to 2820?"

"No, sir, I'm sorry. I don't know where that building is," she replies calmly, continuing to wave cars through.

"What do you mean you don't know?"

"I don't live anywhere near here. I'm filling in today for…"

"I COULDN'T GIVE A CRAP WHERE YOU LIVE OR WHO YOU'RE FILLING IN FOR. AREN'T YOU SUPPOSED TO BE THE AUTHORITY ON STREETS?! YOU'RE WEARING A VEST! YOU'RE STANDING HERE—ON A STREET—WITH THE SOLE PURPOSE REPAIRING THESE ROADS! HOW. HOW CAN YOU POSSIBLY DO THAT WITHOUT KNOWING WHERE YOU ARE AND WHAT'S AROUND YOU?"

"Sir, I'm sorry. I can see you're upset."

"UPSET? I'M NOT UPSET. I'M LOST, AND YOU'RE AN IDIOT. I NEED TO FIND FREAKING 2820. TWO EIGHT TWO ZERO. AND NOW, I'M BACK TO SQUARE ONE. HAVE A GREAT DAY. JERK."

I turn back to my original direction, now ripping mad. She wasn't listening to me. She is just like everyone else in my miserable life. No one can hear me, except my flipping therapist who I have to pay to listen to me. I am silenced and trapped. Trapped in my mind that doesn't work and now trapped on this treadmill that refuses to take me to 2820 Northup Way.

It's 7:30, and there is no way I'm making this appointment on time. But I have to, so I start to run again. As I run I begin to think through a list of excuses and what I'll say to the receptionist. I wonder whether begging is my best option.

I glance up and notice that I am on the side of the street with odd numbers. I need to cross to the other side for even a smidgen of hope that I'll find 2820, even if I am on the wrong street. I don't look. I dash across the street.

Within seconds, a car screeches to a halt, cutting me off. Immediately, I unleash all my anger on the hood of the car, banging it with my fists, powered by pure rage. "You could have killed me!" I snarl. I look up to confront yet another idiot blocking my path. It's only then that I realize I've made a huge mistake.

I'm standing in front of a cop car, my fists firmly planted on the hood.

I am silent as I stare into the officer's eyes. He opens his door and steps slowly out of the car. "Sir," he says, "what's the matter?"

"I need directions. I need to find number 2820, and I've been looking for an hour, and I can't find it, and you almost killed me, which, honestly, may have done me a favor."

"Well, I'm Officer Miller, and as far as I can tell, being lost isn't a reason to run into the street like a lunatic."

"Well, maybe I am a lunatic. I don't know. I was trying to find the office of a doctor who should be able to tell me whether I am or not."

"Where are you going?"

"TO SEE MY PSYCHIATRIST," I yelled.

"A psychiatrist. Sounds like a great idea, sir. Get in the car. I'll take you right now."

Slowly, I release my fists, take my hands off the hood, and circle around to the rear side door. He opens it for me, and I slide into the back seat like a criminal.

Officer Miller slips into the front seat and snaps his belt into place. "Okay, we're heading to 2820 Northup Way?"

"Yes. I mean, I guess. I don't even know if there's a point. I'm late. They told me he won't see me if I'm even a minute late."

"Oh, he'll be seeing you," he said, laughing. "What's your name, sir?"

"Bob, Bob Krulish. Wait." I hesitate. "Why didn't you pull your gun on me or tell me to raise my hands? I could've been some kind of murderous lunatic."

"Well, Bob, not everyone is out to get you. You've got an angel over there on 20th. The road worker there told me there was an upset guy in a red T-shirt who could use some help. When you ran in front of my car and pounded the hood, I knew it was you and that you weren't okay." He shifted in his seat. "I guess sometimes you can just tell when someone really does need a hand."

Hand, I think, H, handshake, hard, hardly, hardened, hatred, hopeless…

The car cruises down the street, and I realize that the road changes its name back to Northup Way in less than two hundred yards from where I saw the road worker. I was so close yet still very lost. It is like I am lost in a terribly cliché metaphor for my entire life.

We pull over unceremoniously at 2820 at exactly 8:20. Officer Miller double-parks, flips on his blue lights, and steps out of the car. He opens my door, motioning for me to step out onto the pavement. I inhale deeply, and my stomach flutters as if a million baitfish are darting back and forth in it.

As we walk up to the building, the doors glide open, the chill of the air conditioning swirls around my body. Officer Miller and I walk in tandem toward the elevator doors, and when they open, I smell the remnants of cologne. We walk up the stairs in silence. Officer Miller casually but confidently walks with me through the office doors and toward the receptionist's desk. His hand is on my back, and we do not stop or pause for a moment.

"The doctor will see Mr. Krulish now," he says, one eyebrow cocked.

"No, sir," the receptionist said. "He's late, so the doctor won't see him today."

"Oh, he'll be seeing him. And he'll be seeing him right now."

Immediately and without question, the elderly receptionist runs out from behind her desk. She knocks on and then begins to open the psychiatrist's heavy wooden door. I push it open, surprised at its weight, and walk away from Officer Miller without looking back.

―――――――

In mere moments I am sitting on a couch that is too soft and staring at Dr. Palmer. He is an older man with white hair, wearing a checkered shirt tucked into Dockers. His belt and shoes look expensive. He sits in an armchair, his legs crossed a little too tightly, and a notebook is balanced on his knee. He clutches his pen in his left hand as he allows the silence to wash over the room.

Left, I think. L, lab, lab test, lab rat, laboratory, labored, labor, late, Linda, Linda, Linda.

269, 221, 2820, numbers, negative, no, no way, never, normal, now...

When he speaks, Dr. Palmer's tone is even. "Bob, where are you right now? Of course, I see you here with me, but where are your thoughts?"

"I don't know how to answer that. They never stay still," I say, shifting in my seat.

"I'm noticing small changes in your face as you sit quietly. I see the signs of racing thoughts, which is what you're describing. Are there patterns?"

"I guess? Yes? My brain tends to chase things. Specifically letters. So, for example…"

"Blueberry," Dr. Palmer interrupts, "blue jay, blue paint, painting, house paint, and so on?"

"Yes. Oh my gosh. Yes."

"Bob, this is not uncommon in a patient like yourself. These are called associative lines of thought and are linked with certain stages and types of mania. As you may know, mania is an element of the disorder I know you are suffering from—severe bipolar 1."

I feel for a moment like someone has come up behind me and squeezed my gut, attempting, but failing at the Heimlich maneuver. This word, bipolar. This is it. The moment that offers a reason, proof that my mind is a jumbled mess. As I let out a sigh of relief, my guard drops and my brain latches on. The elephant races forward.

Bipolar, polar, polar bear, bear, bearings, Bob, Bipolar Bob…

I am talking now, fast—the elephant has its head down, pushing hard against my entire existence. I don't let Dr. Palmer cut in. I let him nod and look at me with a face I appreciate. It is blank, not filled with pity. If anything, his face reflects recognition of everything I say. And for the first time in my life, I feel completely understood.

I tell him everything about the kids, Linda, being misled, having no money, about to be evicted from my apartment. I tell him about the Hummer, the business deals, and the spending. I tell him about my sexual past, the fact that I can drink like a maniac and barely feel a thing. I tell him about my father, his moods, his rhythm, and I cry.

I cry.

Cry, c, crisis, crazy, concerned, capable, compassion, coping…

Then, Dr. Palmer begins to explain. "I know what I'm about to say will sound odd and maybe even dismissive. But none of what you are experiencing is abnormal for someone with this disease, Bob. You are, in fact, one of the lucky ones. From what I can tell and hear in your pressured speech, from what I'm gathering about your trip to my office, you are in what we call a 'mixed state.' What that means is you are suffering from both mania and depression. Let me ask an important question. In the last few years, have you taken medication specifically for depression? An antidepressant perhaps?"

I nod.

"That's what I thought. Prescribed by a GP?"

I nod.

"Do you still take it now?"

I shake my head.

"Did anyone assist you in getting off these medications?"

"No," I whisper.

"This is an extremely serious place you're in. Many antidepressants, especially SSRIs, can cause major complications for those suffering from other, undiagnosed disorders. If there isn't a mood stabilizer in place already, these drugs will always trigger a manic episode in someone with bipolar. These episodes can last anywhere from hours to the full duration of the time you spend on those medications—I mean, years. Then, quitting them cold turkey can throw things into a catastrophic spin. Many, and I mean many do not survive it—the suicide rate for those in your situation is astronomical. Be honest, have you…"

"Yes," I cut in. "I have thought about it. In detail. And tried. Once."

"Okay," Dr. Palmer replies, maintaining his steady composure. "Let's get you sorted out right now."

Within the hour, I have a diagnosis on paper, a written plan in my hands, detailed instructions, a pile of prescriptions, and, for the first time, tangible, real hope. Dr. Palmer's last words to me were a warning.

He told me that if I took my medication, I would eventually be healthy again. But if I did not take my meds, I would end up in one of four places: homeless, hospital, jail or dead and he then said, "I have patients in all four places."

I look down and feel a surge of hope. I am holding the key to making sense of the world again—my golden ticket back into a life that is really my own.

I shake hands with the doctor, give a wave to the receptionist, and leave the office, making my way down the stairs. The papers feel supple and substantial in my hands, and I rub them between my fingers while imagining going home, delivering the news, and putting the puzzle pieces back where they belong. I cross the sleek lobby and step out through the sliding doors, where the hot summer air hugs every inch of my being.

Being, I think, b, baby, babble, babbling, broken, building, bipolar, Bipolar Bob.

Chapter 24

THE BURDEN OF PROOF

My suit is rumpled, my shirt wrinkled, and my tie loosely knotted, but I don't care. I am facing Linda and I now know the reason she was able to get one over on me; it was my mental illness. It's clear that she intends on keeping the settlement agreement as is, even though it means I'm receiving the equivalent of two months of her salary in return for twenty-four years of faithful marriage. She's keeping a small fortune and I'm getting next to nothing.

I sit at the table next to my lawyer, and she sits across from me with hers. Her face looks tighter, glossier, as if she's been injected and scrubbed and polished with the money she's taken from me. It spikes an anger so intense, I want to kick the table over, smash the windows, throw chairs.

"Okay, let's begin," the judge says from the head of the table. She looks at my lawyer. "Do I understand that Mr. Krulish is looking to overturn the settlement agreement he signed seven months ago?"

"Indeed, your honor," my lawyer says.

"On what grounds?" the judge asks. When she smirks, I notice lipstick on her yellowing teeth.

"On the grounds that my client has recently been diagnosed with bipolar 1 disorder and believes he was forced into this decision under false pretenses and when he was not of sound mind due to his bipolar illness," he says.

I strain to hear as Linda whispers to her lawyer, her hands flying as she gesticulates wildly. She slumps back in her chair and her lawyer looks at the judge and says, "Mrs. Krulish would like to make it clear that Mr. Krulish did not have bipolar disorder when he signed the documents in March."

I lean over to my lawyer and whisper-scream, "Take a look at the letter from my doctor, he says I've had it for years. Think about it. She would not have been in the process of divorcing me in the first place if my crazy behavior began only after she asked me to sign this Separation Agreement. It has made life impossible for me and difficult for Linda for months leading up to her decision to kick me out of our home. Otherwise, she never would have done that—come on, you have to see it too! Please, say something!"

My lawyer looks at the letter from my doctor, but motions that we should remain quiet. I look at the judge, watching expectantly, waiting for her to make Linda understand what is happening inside of me; what had happened to us. Instead the judge looked up from the stack of court documents on her desk and stared straight at me for a moment before speaking. "Mr. Krulish, I have read the declarations you submitted from your doctor and therapist regarding your recent diagnosis of bipolar disorder. I have also read the declarations submitted by your wife describing your demeanor closer to the day that you placed your signature on the agreement. It appears from her testimony that you were aware that you were entering into a binding contract with her for the purpose of dividing your marital assets with your wife. According to her testimony, you were given the opportunity to review the agreement with a lawyer, who advised you not to sign it. You chose to sign the agreement anyway. This Court finds that the evidence of the bipolar diagnosis you received almost three months after the fact is insufficient to meet your burden of proving that you lacked the mental capacity to create a binding contract at the time that you signed your Separation Agreement. The Court hereby grants Mrs. Krulish's motion for summary judgement. This case is dismissed."

She stands and leaves, and Linda and her lawyer shuffle papers into their bags and do the same. I am dumbstruck, but I manage to whisper to my lawyer, "What just happened?" "We lost, you're not getting any more of the money, and you just got divorced," he said, all in one breath. Then stood and left me alone in the silence, leaving me to rattle the windows and drive fists into the walls of my mind.

The next day I am sitting in the passenger's seat of Dixon's red Mustang, and we are rumbling down to my apartment. I feel like an inmate being carted to prison. I have started taking handfuls of pills prescribed by Dr. Palmer every night, but so far, there is no change. Pills make me sleep, they get me through the day, but my mind still races, and the anger I feel seeps from my pores.

After the meeting, I went back to my apartment, now certain of my penniless fate. Bishop Johns and Dixon met me, then stood by my side as I explained to my landlord that I had to leave and couldn't pay. The sad look in her eyes gave way to shame that was nearly unbearable. It brings me back to a moment months earlier when I took Noah with me to sell tools at a pawnshop. He looked me in the eyes and said, "You're selling tools for $8 to buy food. Why do you have to do this?"

I hung my head and muttered, "Because I do."

After talking to the landlord today, we went back to my apartment and Dixon and Bishop Johns helped me pack. The bishop knew of people in our church who had a one-hundred-year-old cabin in the woods on a small lake in Sammamish that they were willing to let me stay in. I spent one last night on the floor I'd come to know, tossing and turning, images of fighter jets, fists in walls, and flipping houses racing through my mind. I thought of the apartment, the last thing I even pretended to have, and how I couldn't even hold on to that.

We finally pull up outside the cabin and Dixon and some guys from church help me unpack. Dixon fills the cabinet with basic groceries and the fridge with water and a few perishables, then he leaves. I pace the dirt floor, struck by how it smells like my old rain-soaked couch, and I picture it back on the curb. I take my bag into the bathroom, line my pill bottles up on the sink, then I go outside, wade into the waist-high grass, and scream into the sky, sending birds fleeing for safety.

Chapter 25

TALK ABOUT LOVE

think I've earned the right to be mad. And God doesn't get to escape blame. I devoted so much of my life to Him. I gave more than thirty years of my life to the Mormon Church, showing up, teaching classes, and speaking to my ward often. I lived my life according to His Word, and when I did slip up, I prayed for forgiveness until I was hoarse. Yet, Heavenly Father did nothing to stop Linda from jumping ship when I needed her the most. The Church not only absolved her from this, it seemed at times to cheer her on. Heavenly Father takes it upon Himself to ruin me, ruin everything, and doesn't seem to care about me at all. She has deleted and replaced me with someone new…my kids, my wife, my money—everything I ever cared about is gone. And He gets to sit up there in His throne or whatever while I scream and yell and curse His name? Something about that doesn't seem fair.

I am, for good or bad, still alive. Time has passed in large swathes, and things in my life have ebbed and flowed. The only constants have been church, the blasted parenting plan, treatment, medication, and my frustration with the ongoing battle with Linda. I want out of this ugly pit of self-despair, but I still feel stuck. The hatred pulls me beneath the surface like seaweed wrapped around my ankles. I am grateful that my thoughts have slowed. I can make sense of things, and I'm starting to feel more like myself again—more like myself than I've felt in years. Turns out that the meds and the therapy do work. Yet the piercing, gut-wrenching, overwhelming rage that comes with loss remains. I may not be drowning in mania anymore, but I'm still drowning. Once, Linda had laughed at my diagnosis, brushed it off, characterized it as fiction. But, later, she used it against me, cutting me off even further from the kids. Sometimes, even with slower thoughts, I couldn't stop myself from turning the words of the new parenting agreement over and over in my head. "The father's involvement or conduct may have an adverse effect on the child's best interests because of the factors that follow: A long term emotional or physical impairment, which inter- feres with the performance of parenting functions." It stings to know she'd use something I am wrestling with to rob me of relationships with the most important people in my life. I yearn for my kids with everything I have.

Some moments, the sun peeks through the clouds, and I am able to feel something else. The other day, I was riding the bike I recently got at a secondhand store, and I veered onto a muddy path. I rode past a little girl jumping and splashing in a puddle. She was covered in dirt and purely happy. Instead of cursing her mom for not supervising her kid on a busy bike path or commenting on how the kid should be in school, I laughed. I actually laughed. From the base of my spine to the pit of my stomach, it echoed. I had nearly forgotten the feeling, and it was amaz- ing. That feeling lingered. As I pedaled, I remembered times when my kids and I would fight with Silly String. I remembered the feeling of my lungs burning as I ran toward them, arms wide, scooping them into a hug while my lips curled into a smile.

I realized as I pedaled away from the mom and her daughter that this was what my life had become. Each day I was forced to pedal further and further from my kids. Once, I had seen them every day, then once a week, now just a few hours a few times each month. The court, the Church, Linda, they all worked together to push me away, and soon I was speeding with so much force it was as if I'd been guided downhill. I turned to see the mother and daughter slipping out of view. Then the anger hit me again, hard. The joy receded into the blackness, leaving only cruel and bitter criticism.

I am seething, stewing in constant, hungry hatred that makes me want to punch holes in things. Nowhere is that darkness more startlingly obvious than within the walls of my church. Now, palms cold and sweaty, I sit in the bishop's office in my new ward, in Bothell, thirty miles away from my old ward, for our weekly meeting. I feel small, huddled on a plush velvet couch. The bishop looks across at me from his office chair, which makes him look assured and normal-sized. I think it's intentional.

For weeks, the bishop has been listening to me talk about how much I hate God and how stupid church is and how badly I want out. I've tried everything to get under his skin so he forces me out the door, but nothing has worked thus far. Sometimes I just sit in his office and tell him about all the ways I feel like a failure. Other times, I talk about Heavenly Father and say as many vile things as I can, but the bishop just sits there listening. Only once have I seen him react, and it was barely noticeable. Back in October, his eyebrow flickered ever so slightly, indicating that I may have suggested that God was a motherless idiot one time too many. But today, as usual, the bishop is stone-faced, and I am ripping mad, finishing a rant about everyone who has wronged me.

"Doesn't it exhaust you to hate? You hate so hard and with your whole heart. Don't you just want to take a break?" the bishop asks.

"A break?" I snap. "You don't get a break when you're crazy. And it isn't hard for me to hate people who deserve it. Look at my life right now."

"I see your life. And I see someone trapped in a pattern of hatred and self-loathing that bleeds into everything. You can change this."

"I can't change this. I have a medical condition. I'm different than you, different than everyone under this roof."

"Yes, that may be true. But, remember, you're still relatively new to this ward. No one here knows your past."

"You don't think people talk? This isn't a desert island." I settle back into the couch with a sigh. "People talk, text, email, whatever. There's no way no one in here knows what happened. There's not a chance that people don't gossip about me, my kids, my…"

The bishop presses on. "You have a place to live, people who love you despite what is happening inside you, and a Heavenly Father who will not give up on you. No matter what you do, what you say, and how many times you say it. I think you owe it to yourself to try to make a change."

"God doesn't care about me. And I don't owe anyone anything."

"Okay, how about this? What if we start with something safe to move you toward healing?"

"I hate that word."

"Healing?"

"Safe," I respond with disgust. "There's no such thing."

"Okay, let me start again. It's been a long time. I'm afraid that if you stay in this place of anger much longer, it will eat you alive. I want to offer you a chance to speak to the ward."

"Why would I do that?" I blurt, louder than I intended.

The bishop calmly responds, "You're here. You keep coming here. If your heart were completely black, totally shut off from us, from Him, you wouldn't be here. So how about you put the brooding aside for a day and get back into this community? You used to love speaking."

"What do you want me to speak about? Want me to educate on the benefits of telling Heavenly Father that He's useless? Because I can do that in my sleep."

Without missing a beat the bishop says, "I was thinking you could talk about love."

"You've got to be kidding me," I say, laughing.

"No, I'm not, actually. I think you owe it to yourself and others to explore the opposite side of what you've allowed yourself to become the past few years."

"I haven't allowed anything. This happened to me," I insist.

"Things happen to us. They do," the bishop says, his tone measured. "And they can be hard. But how we react and how we let that affect our lives is our choice. In the end, you can choose whether to stay in this place of anger, slowly losing more and more until you no longer exist. Or you can pick yourself up and do something about it." The bishop makes it all sound so easy.

"What I want to do about it is tell everybody in this building that they are a bunch of losers, judgmental hypocrites, liars."

"Well, I'm not sure that's the direction I'd go with the talk, but if that's what you feel called to do, by all means. I do think you have it in you to show people that you have something to offer. I believe in you."

"You believe in me? Do you work for Hallmark now, Bishop?" I push, trying to get a reaction out of the bishop, even a tiny one.

But he continues, "You've made it this far. Just push a little harder. Do something that scares you."

"I wake up every day. THAT scares me," I snap back. "I'm not afraid to speak in front of the ward. You just have to know that there's a chance I could get up there and call everyone out on their crap."

"Despite what you may think, I know you. And I don't think that's what you'll do."

"But I might."

"You might."

I take a deep breath and decide that if I have to do this, I will tell my ward exactly how I feel.

When I left the meeting with the bishop last Tuesday, I had an emotional breakdown. I ran out of the building and jumped into my car and sped toward home, fueled by anger that I had committed to speaking. My lungs screamed as I rode into the sunset yelling and cursing. The bishop loved to remind me that I was "new to the ward," that this was a "fresh start," but that seemed totally off base. There was enough crossover between wards and the story of my fall from grace was so melodramatic that it was impossible to believe it wasn't fodder for the bored.

Back home, I sat outside in my car and yelled for an hour, trying to figure out what I could possibly say about love when I didn't love anyone and no one loved me. Instead of planning, I told God to buzz off and pushed the whole thing aside until my ride to church today. I stopped on the path, sat on a bench, and jotted down some ideas.

Now, I'm sitting at the front of the sprawling chapel, and I feel nothing. I want to be scared. I want to be excited. I want to be something, but I sit, stiff and controlled, every muscle in my body flexed. I am ready to speak to a roomful of people, people who I think are cruel hypocrites. Over the last year, I have wished for terrible things to happen to the worst of them.

Before I walk up to the pulpit, I stare out into the crowd. There are about three hundred people in the room, and I know in my gut that they have all heard what I've been through. They know all about my family.

They know of me, but they don't know me. So this is my chance to reclaim some part of this one-sided narrative. Now, if I make myself look like an idiot, at least it will be my doing.

I take my place behind the pulpit and draw a breath. I stare at the microphone, which looks like a sad black lollipop, and wait for the crowd to quiet. I begin, "Hello. My name is Bob Krulish, and I've been asked to speak about love"—I clear my throat—"and I'm going to talk about ten things that I would need to do if I felt like being loving." I pause for effect, then continue, "The problem is, I don't feel like being loving."

I pause for another moment, and the crowd seems uncomfortable. I relish in it, letting it linger just a little longer. Then I continue, "I don't have any problem with crowds. I just hate the people."

I take a shorter pause this time and go on. "As a matter of fact, I don't like anybody in this room."

The crowd begins to laugh, easing the tension. I add, pointing arbitrarily around the room, "Seriously. I don't like you. Or you. I don't even know why you're here." I glance at the bishop, whose face is blank. I carry on. "As a matter of fact, I wrote down ten ways to be more loving, but because I don't like you and I don't know you, I'm only going to give you three of them, and you will have to figure out the other seven on your own." I place foreboding emphasis on the word own.

There is more laughter. I keep going. "I'm not kidding. In fact, I promise. I'm the guy who gets on an airplane and puts on his big headphones and gives other passengers dirty looks, like 'Don't talk to me! I don't want to hear about your life. I don't give a crap about your life.'" The crowd laughs harder this time, and I begin to feel energized, "The truth is that I hate people because I have an illness. But I don't want to get into that."

The crowd continues to rumble with chuckles and whispers, and I am suddenly hit with the unavoidable urge to say more. I clutch the sides of the pulpit, my knuckles white, palms clammy. I recognize this as a spirit prompting. I know it so deeply that I give in to the tension. I look far into the crowd for a moment and notice a woman with tear-stained cheeks and a look of distress on her face. I add, "It's kind of a serious illness that keeps me from liking people."

Then, I feel the nudging inside me grow so intense that I am almost unable to control what will come out of my mouth. It is as if I'm being shoved by two hands—they are inching me toward a cliff—and I blurt, "Okay, the reason I don't like people is that I have bipolar disorder."

And with that, there are crickets. Babies are still. Kids are no longer playing in the back. There isn't a rustle of paper or the creak of a pew. I pray for a tornado or an earthquake or an elephant to escape from the zoo and trample the place, leaving blood and guts on the walls and crisp white paper flying, but there is nothing.

The bishop's lips curl into a smile.

The silence is pure.

<hr>

The rest of the talk goes smoothly. I use a technique I have relied on for years. I start with a topic, then a single Scripture verse, then I let things flow. One verse always leads to another, then another. As I map out a talk, I always feel I could cap it at any time or keep going into infinity, letting the Apostles do the work for me. Only now do I realize this may have been my first encounter with healthy associative thinking, letting one small thought trigger a waterfall of information I could actually put to good use.

Even though it feels good to have engaged a crowd, I feel miserable. I am completely exposed, as if I just stood naked in front of the entire ward. I'm watching people file out now, and I am frozen to my seat. I can't gauge their reactions. I can't tell whether they think I'm sick or dangerous. Anxiety sits in the pit of my stomach like a block of ice and slowly climbs toward my throat, threatening to choke me out. I can't believe the bishop made me do that. Nor can I stand how happy he is that I have basically revealed every inch of myself to the gossip-hungry masses. Now, not only am I the poor, sad guy whose life is completely and utterly ruined, I'm the guy with a mental illness. Perfect. People who didn't hate me before will definitely hate me now. I shake my head dismissively at Heavenly Father as I stand to leave, ready to go home and curse Him for forcing me to tell everyone that I am crazy. I decide that the bishop is a complete moron and that I'm done with him for good.

As I push through the double doors, the sunlight hits me and I can almost taste the fresh air. To my left, I notice a woman standing against the wall, and I can tell she wants to talk to me. I glance at her again and realize it is the woman I noticed in the crowd with the tear-stained cheeks. I don't want to hear what she has to say. I just want to bolt. I walk faster, pretending not to see her.

"Hi, I just wanted to say thank you for that," she calls to me, walking quickly with her hand out.

I can't avoid her now. I stop and take her hand, giving it a quick shake, and reply, "I mean, I really just told a room full of people that I hate them. Then, I told them a hugely embarrassing secret about myself. But you're welcome." I turn to leave.

"Wait, don't go. I just need one second. You have to know that what you just did means a lot to me"—she sniffs—"to be honest, I'm still shaking."

"Maybe you should eat something."

"No, I mean, I was so moved by what you said. This isn't my normal ward. It's not close to anything. I don't even know why I chose to come here, but this morning, I missed the service at my ward because I was dropping my husband off at a treatment facility."

A wave of discomfort crashes over me as she begins to cry, and I offer only, "I'm sorry."

"Don't be. He's safe. We're safe, and everyone is okay. But, I mean, I had to bring him to an institution. He had a manic break. It was so severe, unlike anything I'd ever seen. He…" She trails off.

"Let me guess," I interrupt to let her regroup. "He said a bunch of crazy stuff? Maybe took off his clothes? Pounded on walls? Screamed and cursed?"

"Something like that." She continues talking. "I was broken by it. I came today just to pray for him, for healing. And seeing you up there, hearing you talk, seeing a person who is well with this illness is the first bit of hope I've had that my husband might be well someday."

I force myself to look into the woman's glassy eyes, and I am dumbstruck. How could someone as broken as me give someone like this hope? In the depths of my soul I am desperately sad. And I am angry—deeply, passionately, fully, and completely angry. All of these things come from the fact that I have lost things I love. And this woman, eyes brimming with tears, shaking and sad, has seen something in me that is not broken but fixed.

I say, "Listen, your husband, he loves you. He loves your kids. None of this is about that. I know you must be feeling…maybe like you could have done or said something to make it different? But you couldn't have. It's chemicals. Your husband and me. We're messed up in the head. But you did the right thing taking him to get help." I swallow hard.

"Thank you for saying that. I'm glad I came here. Your family must be proud of you."

With a half-smile, I turn to leave. She has no idea what they feel. She's one of a small group who hasn't heard the gossip and doesn't know what a mess things are for me. She can't understand what fuels my anger, what makes me feel the way I do. She doesn't know about my kids, how awesome they are, how I love them with every fiber of my being, and how I lost them. She doesn't know how wonderful my life has been and what I lost because I am, apparently, crazy. And suddenly I realize, I feel love.

———

When I get to my house, there is a box waiting on the front porch. I don't even go into the house. I tear at the tape with my bare hands, picking, pulling, and tugging until the box is open. Inside, there is a mesh bag filled with twenty footballs and two clear plastic packages, one containing netting, the other containing plastic rods. Immediately, I get to work snapping the rods together and pulling the netting in place. Once it's assembled, I step back and smile at the training target that sits in front of a spindly elderberry bush.

I drag the bag of balls from the porch and place it next to me about twenty feet away from the target. I pick up a ball and throw it. I miss. I do it again and again, drilling some and missing others. Once I've thrown all the balls, I pick up the empty mesh bag, head to the target, and collect them all. Then I drag it back to my spot and start again. With every throw, I think of Logan. I think about how I'm improving myself to match his skill level. Because in the light of day I see that Logan isn't a little me—he is himself. Now, almost a man, he is someone who makes me proud. For the first time, in the silence of my mind, I can feel the pull to know my kids and to love them well. To wrap them in my arms, smile slyly, and watch as they run through the grass, darting bright, swirling Silly String as I spray it in their direction. They might be older now, but it doesn't matter. They need me and I need them. I grip the pebbly leather of the ball, wind up, and throw with a wobbly flick of the wrist.

———

It is Saturday and I arrive at our meeting place with two large pizzas. Because of the parenting plan, drawn up by Linda's lawyer, I can only meet the kids at houses of families from their ward and never see them without supervision. I can't speak to them outside of this time either, so the total time allotted for me to know and love my kids amounts to a measly seventy-two hours per year. It's hard for me to process; they are teenagers now, but I know I have to accept it if I want to be with them at all. I feel the anger swell, but it passes quickly in a tiny, fleeting wave.

As I walk up the path to the front door I hear birds chirping, neighbor children laughing, a bike bell in the distance. I notice now that living in the present is a gift. I am awake to the beauty of the world. I can see things, smell things, experience things that I used to miss time and time again as I lived in the war zone that was my mind.

The host family was there, but I knew I'd barely see them. I knew I was there just to meet the kids in the backyard for a quick bite. I rang the bell with my foot, jostling the pizzas in my hands, which were still piping hot. Holly answered the door, and I walked in, waving to the family, who were playing Jenga on the coffee table. I walked through their house, walls covered in glossy, professional pictures and drawings scribbled by little ones. We moved through the kitchen, which smelled like apple pie.

In the yard, Logan and Noah sat at the table and jumped up to give me a hug—Amanda is off at school now. When they sat, I was struck by the fact that there were no dangling feet or highchairs anymore. They sat like grown-ups, crossed legs, bright eyes, all engaged in deep conversation about life, current events, boyfriends, girlfriends, gossip. As we finished the pizza, I noticed a football on the ground, stood, and scooped it up.

"Wanna toss a few before you head out?" I ask.

The kids jump up and scatter in the yard. I point at Logan, who runs far. I wind up and expertly toss a pass his way. I am delighted as it leaves my hand and spins exactly the way I'd practiced. He catches it, winces at his stinging hands, then throws it back. Holly and Noah cheer. I wind up and throw it to him again. He catches it and exclaims, "Whoa, Dad! These passes are awesome!"

"Thanks, man!" I say. "I'm still practicing."

"Well," he says with a smile, "you don't need to practice anymore. You've got this, Pops."

The courtroom is quiet, except for the shuffling of paper and murmurs. I adjust my weight in my seat as she finishes what she wanted to say and returns to her seat next to Linda. I glance at Linda as the judge jots something on a piece of paper. I know the woman I used to love is somewhere in there beneath her thick, shiny veneer, but I can't see her anywhere. She is distant, removed, as if the parts of her I cared for so deeply have evaporated over time.

When the judge finally looks up, I instinctively look down to straighten my rumpled clothes. My hands land on my starched tie and I realize today, no tugging is necessary to make myself look presentable. My clothes aren't rumpled like they used to be. My suit is pressed, my shirt ironed, and my hair neatly trimmed. I am here, present and engaged.

"Mr. Krulish," the judge begins, "I have taken time to review the parenting plan that was put in place between you and Ms. Krulish. It is the court's finding that restrictions this stringent are not necessary or appropriate given the very clear improvements you have made, the glowing reports of the supervisors and your clinical team, including your continued close monitoring of your psychiatric condition. This court hereby rejects the lower court's ruling. The parenting plan is hereby overturned and you have the apologies of this court for all your trouble, Mr. Krulish.

I sat for a moment completely stunned. Linda's face didn't change; she simply gathered her things and left the room. I shook hands with my lawyer, my eyes brimming with tears. Then I stood up and walked out of the courtroom feeling as if heavy shackles had just been removed from my limbs. I cannot believe how much time with my children I have sacrificed and how this dragged on for six long years for Logan and me.

The sun was shining when I stepped outside. I stopped on the courthouse steps and drew a breath, noticing the various calls of birds singing in the distance. I pictured hugging each of my kids one by one, looking into their eyes, telling them how much I love them. I opened my eyes, jogged down the stairs, and headed for home, planning to cook a celebratory dinner. I thought about ingredients as a salty Seattle breeze rustled the leaves of the trees lining the walkway, thinking through the steps of making my famous meatballs. As I pictured the smell of fresh garlic filling my kitchen, I let myself enjoy something totally new to me: a mind that no longer screams—it only whispers.

EPILOGUE

I n the process of writing this book, I've had to relive some of the most challenging experiences of my life. It's been difficult not only to review events that were inherently traumatizing but to take a hard look at things I didn't even realize were traumatizing at the time. To me, that level of crazy was just normal. As I began to research for the book, I started to dig into my own life more critically than ever before. I discovered that there were a lot of episodes throughout my lifetime that were pretty dramatic, when I looked like a bit of a jerk, many, many different times, and it was always when I was manic. Looking at my life objectively, I now realize that I have likely upset a lot of people. To those of you who are reading this, I hope you know how sorry I am. It was my illness that was taking me away—it was the force behind my behavior. It's hard to look back and see how much of a jerk I was and how many times I hurt people, how many bad things I said and did and how disruptive I was to my relationships with the people I love the most. I've had to push past the shame to publish this book in hopes of preventing others from being taken down by this, the disease of loss.

Today, I am happy to say that things are very good for me. After some six hundred hours of therapy and more than sixty adjustments to the medications (during the past ten years), I finally found the right combination of medications, therapy, etc. that leaves me healthy and thriving. I have work that I like to do, coaching families and individuals on how to live well with bipolar disorder. I am in a very special relationship with somebody that I love so much and she loves me.

As hard as all this has been, I would say that the struggles I've been through as a result of my disorder have taught me to be a better person. I have a huge amount of empathy for people who are struggling and I'm able to put into words what they are going through. This allows me to bridge the gap between people suffering with bipolar and their family members. I coach families as they come to me looking for support. Together, we take the time to learn about bipolar disorder and not only educate ourselves about the illness but critically talk through how to treat and manage it. I teach suffering individuals coping skills that make it possible to live healthier and happier. And then most importantly, I teach the family communication skills, the importance of keeping stress away from the bipolar individual, and other ways to keep him or her as asymptomatic as possible. I wish I could have been there for my own family and spared them all this pain, but I was just too sick to do anything about it.

If you are struggling, please know that although it will take time to get yourself feeling better, it will happen. It will just take time and a real concerted effort. They key is to get help soon as possible and to focus your energy on finding a team of licensed professionals who can facilitate treatment and the ongoing management of your disease. You'll want to consult a psychiatrist and a therapist, ideally two professionals who will communicate with one another, forming a team that will work to get you well. And when you do see these clinicians, honesty is key. These professionals rely upon you self-reporting your symptoms rather than your blood tests. They're relying upon how you report what your experiences really are. If you're worried about being able to honestly report all of your symptoms, bring a family member or your significant other to the appointment with you. The more honest information the doctor has, the better treatment you're going to get.

Many people tell me that they're concerned about taking meds. They fear they'll lose a part of themselves, that they'll become totally numb, that life will never look the same. Those ideas scare them enough to where they're willing to allow bipolar disorder to systematically destroy their lives. The truth is, if you're in the throes of battling bipolar disorder without medication, you're not really your true self. Maybe you've never been your true self, nor have you seen what your true potential is. When you can restore your mind, reorganize your thoughts, and think clearly, that's where you really realize your true self—your really good, healthy, true self. I don't think anybody's true self is somebody who is not properly treated.

If you have a family member who is suffering, please don't lose hope. They need you to pursue treatment on their behalf, hold their hand, keep things calm, and continue the fight. Please offer to attend appointments with them, pick up prescriptions, and hold them accountable for keeping up with management of the disorder. Most importantly, know that your loved one deeply loves and cares for you—he or she is just sick. There is a big difference between the illness and the person. Please do all you can to separate the two. There is always hope for healing. I am living proof of that.

I always say that there's a Bob and there's a Bipolar Bob. Bipolar Bob is mischievous. He can get me into all kinds of trouble. And so, every day I've got to keep Bipolar Bob down by doing the right stuff, using my coping strategies, staying away from stressful things, staying on my meds, and seeing my doctor and therapist. By doing that, every morning I wake up and I kick Bipolar Bob's behind, knock him down, and put him under my foot. I drag Bipolar Bob around with me, never taking my foot off. At first, as I learned the ropes, it felt like a chore. Now it's just a part of who I am. And it'll soon be a part of who you are too.

My biggest hope for you, my friend, is that you find the healing you deserve. If you are the one who is suffering, please hear me that you can live a healthy, happy life. It's a matter of finding and working the right treatment and letting loved ones support you in your healing journey. Without treatment, I've destroyed and lost everything in my life over and over again. With treatment, I've been able to have the things that I want, and you can too.

In time, you end up finding a new relationship to your feelings. They are no longer huge, sweeping forces that swoop down and shake things up. They are subtler, allowing you to experience them without completely losing yourself in them. Soon, euphoria is replaced with real, true happiness and joy, which is far safer to experience. I'll tell you one thing. A happy, content person might leave a meeting and swing by a drive-thru and grab an ice cream to celebrate. He's sure not going to whip out his phone and try like I did to buy a helicopter.

The truth is, if it is possible for me to manage my disorder, it's possible for anyone. What I've done can be done by anybody. I'm not special. I don't feel like this is a story that is impossible for other people to achieve. I think what I've done with my story here is showed the struggle. But what I want to emphasize over and over again is that it really is just a matter of the proper medication from a psychiatrist, therapy from a psychologist or a licensed therapist along with a healthy set of coping skills.

Please hear me when I say, you can live successfully with this disorder. We live with it. We learn to ride the waves. We learn to make it work in our favor. After a while, the disorder stops looking like the enemy. Once you learn how to control it and harness it, things start to get better and better. You can have a family, you can have a marriage, you can have relationships, you can have a job, you can have a career, you can have a house, you can have a boat, you can have a car. You can have all the things that everyone else has. Eventually, you may even see the disease as a gift. Our human experience is just so unique and runs the gambit that most people can't grasp. Our worlds are bigger than theirs. Our imaginations are bigger. Our experiences are bigger. The way they get processed in our mind, it's all big, big, big, big. The treatment will never take that away. You'll always have bipolar. You are always capable of those highs and lows, but the treatment allows you to better operate, preventing you from destroying your life and hurting the people you love most. Find your treatment, find your coping skills, find your way.

ACKNOWLEDGEMENTS

Many thanks and all my love to the love of my life Leslie Wallis who has always believed in the value of my story. I can never thank you enough.

All my thanks and love to my children and my grandchildren who inspire me to get well and stay well.

Many thanks to Kenneth for always being there.

Loving thanks to a mom who taught me how to love and never gave up on me.

A special thanks to Glen, Dixon, Kyle and Wayne for the support you gave me when everything in my life fell apart.

Thank you, David and Megan for providing me with a roof over my head when I had none.

I can't thank my co-author, Alee Anderson, enough. She too lives a life with bipolar and was able to accurately articulate just how the bipolar brain thinks. Thank you Alee!

Thank you, Tony Robbins, who taught me how to build the massive action plan I created to wellness. You saved my life and helped me build an incredible one.

Dr. Joshua Bess, my psychiatrist, for your exceptional care and spot on recommendations.

Janina Johnson, my therapist who taught me a better way to think.

Dr. Xavier Amador for the wonderful foreword and your LEAP program. You are saving people by the thousands!

My editor, Elizabeth Bruce as the masterful wordsmith who smoothed out the kinks.

Kevin Anderson and Cole Gustafson for your enthusiasm for my story.

My publisher, David Hancock at Morgan James for your belief in my story and Gayle West and Jim Howard and everyone else at Morgan James for their talent and creativity.

The National Alliance on Mental Illness, especially the local affiliates

The friends, and even strangers, that offered me their support and did not judge me without knowing my story.

ABOUT THE AUTHOR

During Bob Krulish's tenure at Nationwide Insurance and Safeco, he saw a doctor for stress related symptoms and was incorrectly diagnosed with depression. He was placed on a medication that would ultimately cause him to ruin his own life. Once Bob received the proper diagnosis of Bipolar 1 Disorder, he was able to slowly put his life back together and soon found the strength to share his struggles with others. Now, he coaches private clients and their families to better manage the disorder. Through his teaching, he seeks to eliminate the suffering caused by bipolar disorder.

Bob holds a national certification from the Copeland Center to teach their Wellness Recovery Action Plan Course anywhere in the United States. He teaches the In Our Own Voice Program in Washington State through the National Alliance on Mental Illness (NAMI) and has served on the board of directors for NAMI Eastside. Additionally, Bob is certified through Dr. Xavier Amador's LEAP Institute to teach their programs nationally.

He is currently developing a robust online program including webinars, written, and audio content as a pioneer in the field of mental illness. Through this work, he continues to build his platform and speak at national conferences about hope and recovery. Bob currently lives just outside of Seattle, WA. Please visit bobkrulish.com to learn more.